When Will You Find Love?

Your astrological guide to when, where
and who you'll love

When Will You Find Love?

Your astrological guide to when, where
and who you'll love

Orli Lysen

Winchester, UK
Washington, USA

First published by Dodona Books, 2014
Dodona Books is an imprint of John Hunt Publishing Ltd., Laurel House, Station Approach,
Alresford, Hants, SO24 9JH, UK
office1@jhpbooks.net
www.johnhuntpublishing.com
www.dodona-books.com

For distributor details and how to order please visit the 'Ordering' section on our website.

Text copyright: Orli Lysen 2013

ISBN: 978 1 78099 532 8

A CIP catalogue record for this book is available from the British Library.

Design: Stuart Davies

Printed in the USA by Edwards Brothers Malloy

We operate a distinctive and ethical publishing philosophy in all
areas of our business, from our global network of authors to
production and worldwide distribution.

CONTENTS

For DB, PB and Ixchel

Introduction

When will you find love?

You don't need to have been cheated, mistreated, lied to or made blue to want some real, honest to goodness love and romance in your life.

If you keep meeting the wrong kind of partner, or no partner at all, and you're tired of leaving things to chance and want to take control of your love life, you've come to the right place.

This book aims to show you not only when you'll meet your true love, but also where you're likely to meet him or her, as well as what he or she will be like, so you'll recognize your partner-to-be as soon as your paths cross.

You might be wondering how can this possibly work as isn't astrology all down to fate? In fact it's all down to cycles which repeat over and over again, with slight variations that make things more (or less) favorable to achieving the romantic outcome you want.

For instance Mars, the planet of passion and one that's very helpful in working out timings for relationships, is in exactly the same place only once every two years for about eight weeks, so miss that and it could potentially mean a two year wait until your next window of opportunity for romance.

Even the love planet Venus, which you can usually count on in the lottery of love, gets temperamental at times, heading backwards (or retrograde) to throw a cosmic spanner in the works.

But there are in-between times when the quest for true love all works out beautifully.

With a few easy-to-follow guidelines, you can pinpoint these to help put you in the right place at the right time to meet your love match.

There's the potential for love in everyone's future, but it can take a while for circumstances to be just right. There's no point simply sitting at home waiting for love to come knocking on your door. That might just happen, and you might well fall for the TV repair man or the person who delivers your pizza, but it's much more likely to occur if you pursue some of the options outlined in the chapters for your sign. These will put you in the perfect place and the right mindset for the right person to connect with you when the timing is also spot on.

So in the meantime you need to get in touch with what you love. Dress up, put more effort into your friendships and personal pleasures, and fill your life with beauty and happy experiences each day. Nothing is more attractive than a person who's already fulfilled. Who would you rather date: Someone who's waiting for someone else to come along to make them happy, or someone who's genuinely in love with their life and radiating joy?

Live your life to the fullest. Be interesting, be interested and you'll be working with the planets to help you meet your ideal partner. Putting your life on hold if your ideal astro love time is months away is letting yourself down and not taking advantage of the planetary energies that want you to develop to be the kind of person your ideal partner is looking for too.

Sometimes this will mean stepping out of your comfort zone and trying something different, or finding yourself in a place you'd never normally consider going to, but that's how the magic happens. If you always do the same thing, the same way, you'll always meet the same kind of lover, so you'll go through the same kinds of situations you've always been through, leaving you frustrated, loveless and back where you started.

Now's your chance to take control of your love life.

And if you think you must be getting a little desperate or crazy to consult the stars to find true love, think again. Back in the day (we're talking 16th century) astrology was highly regarded and almost exclusively for society's elite, for royalty and for the important decision-makers of the time. The finest minds in the land would use their knowledge of the movements of the planets to select the most beneficial timings for major events.

Queen Elizabeth the First's coronation date was specifically chosen by the Royal Astrologer, Dr John Dee, to take place on 15th January 1559, and she went on to become one of the most powerful and revered monarchs of all time. There wasn't a lot of romance for Good Queen Bess, the virgin queen, however, as her specially chosen day was all about her career. But your special days will be all about your love life.

While the key point here is that each sign of the zodiac has opportunities when love and the chances of meeting that special someone are higher than at other times, it's worth also realizing that your true romance might not be with the kind of person or Sun sign you'd normally fall for, so keep an open mind.

You may have read that if you're an Earth sign, pleasure-loving Taurus for example, you'll get on best with the other Earth signs, meticulous Virgo and sensible Capricorn. The same goes for the Air signs and it's true there are compatibilities for quick-thinking Gemini, stylish Libra and quirky Aquarius. If you're a Fire sign you'll share certain qualities with action-oriented Aries, limelight-loving Leo and adventurous Sagittarius. And if you're ruled by Water you may have an emotional connection with nurturing Cancer, mysterious Scorpio and intuitive Pisces. Certainly you'll have something in common with those signs who share your element, but that doesn't necessarily mean they'll be a match made in the heavens.

There's so much more to it all than just your Sun sign and your element, and you're about to see how loving Venus, passionate Mars and lucky planet Jupiter's influence will improve your chances of finding true love too.

Using this book you'll be activating your romance zone (or 5th house), which in the world of astrology relates to romance, engagements and taking a risk or a gamble, in this case, on love.

It's easy and more effective than you can imagine. And you don't need to be an astrology expert to understand it and make it work.

Think of it as the love equivalent of being on a diet without having to eat less or exercise more!

And don't worry either if you've loved and lost before. You may have thought that he or she was 'the one', but at different times in your life a different kind of partner can suit you more than someone you thought was just your type, or even your soulmate. Be open to new experiences and again you'll increase your chances of finding someone who's right for you, right now and forever.

So does this really work? I tested the theory on myself and was amazed to find that the most important and long-lasting relationship I've had was with a Gemini guy I met while producing a book, working in the offices of a former school. Gemini rules literature (books) and education (school), and my Venus sign is Gemini. The day we met we were both in a strong Venus cycle (an age that's a multiple of 7) and Venus and Mars were close together (or conjunct) in the skies, which is one of the best times of all for a relationship to start. We were together for 14 years and are still very good friends.

I looked into this further and found that each key relationship in my life started when Venus and Mars were locked in an astrological embrace.

Astrology worked for me and I'm going to show you how it can work for you. So let's get started, as timing is everything!

For simplicity, I've referred to partners as male but everything here relates to your ideal partner, whether male or female. Additionally, a small number of the activities suggested are quite adventurous so make sure you're physically able before trying them out. Low impact alternatives are suggested and work equally well.

How to Use This Book

Six Simple Steps to Discover When You'll Find Love

1. Read the chapter on your Sun sign to find out about your love style and WHERE you're most likely to meet the love of your life.

2. Check the Venus lists to find your Venus sign and discover WHO your Venus sign says is most suitable for you.

3. Check whether you're in a strong Venus cycle.

4. Find out when Jupiter is making you lucky in love.

5. Check the dates when Venus and Mars are together in your Sun sign, your Romance sign and your Relationship sign.

6. Then use the pages at the back of the book to note these key places, people and times and put it all together to find out WHEN you'll find true love.

Chapter 1

Where to Find Love if You're Aries

As an Aries, you're probably used to reading that your key trait is to act first and think later. At work or in an emergency this is an admirable quality and gets things moving while others are still wondering what on earth they should be doing.

But if you find this full-on approach slips over into your romantic life this could be the reason you haven't yet found your soulmate.

Arranging to date seemingly cute guys without getting to know them a little first can mean you encounter a whole bunch of unsuitable candidates (or just plain crazies) in the love stakes, which could be enough to put you off the idea of romance altogether. It's a little like sticking a pin in a map to work out where to go on vacation. You might end up in a tropical paradise, but you could just as easily land in a war-torn disaster zone.

It doesn't have to be that way. Your key to finding love that lasts is to take a step back from the brink just as you're about to hurl yourself into the unknown.

Love (and life) isn't necessarily all about action and adrenaline, but neither does it have to be tedious and routine, which would be the ultimate turn-off for you.

This time around you're going to approach romance to get results that sparkle bright enough to light up the entire night sky, not fizzle out like a firework that's failed to launch.

If you've always gone for the quieter type of guy so that you're not overshadowed it's time to find a man with a larger personality who challenges you, as you're quite a combative, competitive person. Your 'first impressions' approach to life and love can mean that in the past you've been drawn to men who, while they may look amazing because attractiveness is a high priority for you, may have turned out to be not quite so amazing underneath as you'd hoped or imagined. Their saving grace may have been the fact that they let you take the lead in most if not all situations.

But because you're independent and used to making your own (often snap) decisions, a lover who can match you in every way or even outdo you is more likely to keep you fascinated and stand the test of time.

He'll have his own ideas and opinions and won't be too timid to voice them, even if they don't happen to coincide with yours. Rather than someone who says yes to you just to keep the peace, he'll enjoy the fun of challenging you, with a smile, just to have the pleasure of keeping you on your toes.

Your sign tends to prefer the thrill of the chase and gets easily bored or even loses interest when things and people become too predictable and complacent. No chance of this with the man who's truly right for you. It might feel like a tug-of-war at times but as Aries is ruled by warrior planet Mars you'll enjoy the kind of verbal sparring that ends in laughter and passion.

This could be the soulmate connection you've been looking for. But the man for you is not necessarily the one you carry a picture of in your head so be open to new experiences, new sensations and new opportunities in your quest for love. As you thrive on being the first to try anything new, this approach should very definitely be your thing.

So where do you find this miracle man? In places you may have overlooked before, and in others that may never even have crossed your mind.

1. Get Dramatic

Being an Aries means there's always a part of you that loves to take center stage, whether it's at work where you like to be the decision-maker, or in your personal life where you tend to be the leader of the gang.

Even if this doesn't sound totally like you, and that will

depend on your individual astrological chart, there's definitely some area of life where you like to take the leading role.

So in your quest for love think about joining your local amateur dramatic society and auditioning for the lead in their next production. There's no better way to expand your dating pool than getting together with others on your wavelength, with the added bonus of actually enjoying yourself into the bargain.

And the odds are good that you'll win the heart of someone either working on the production or watching the show who'll want you to be his real-life leading lady.

Acting can also be a means of 'getting out of your own way'. So if you're always the feisty one, which your sign does tend to be, try a softer and gentler role for a change. Or vice versa. You might get to like it, finding that it brings out hidden layers that you either didn't know you had or that you just don't let others see enough of.

If being in front of a crowd doesn't appeal, try organizing the publicity, being in charge of the box office or refreshments, or even heading up the whole production as director which may be even more your style.

Your key word for finding love is 'drama'. Not as in making a drama out of a crisis, but definitely by adding an element of fantasy into your life.

You could join a theater club to get hot tickets to the latest shows, or arrange theater outings with friends, but do it on a big scale that attracts friends of friends too. Hire a chauffeur-driven limo, act like you're attending an awards ceremony and really make a night of it.

It's not even just about the show, it's about being in the spotlight, thinking outside your usual dating scenarios and putting yourself in the right kind of place to get noticed and get connected.

How might this work romantically? You could hook up with a theater producer, or with the cute guy selling programs who's also the understudy for the leading actor.

You could get into conversation with the gorgeous guy sitting next to you who doesn't even like the theater and is there because a friend made him go, so meeting you turns his whole evening into something special and makes yours even better too.

If you're at a movie, you might spill your popcorn over a complete stranger at a tense moment and laugh about it with him as the lights go up later and end up hooking up (this did actually happen to an Aries friend of mine). It really is all about being in the right place at the right time, then letting the astrology work its magic.

2. Get In Touch With Your Inner Child

There's something about the Aries sense of humor that taps right back into childhood. It's likely that you've never quite outgrown the things that made you smile when you were growing up so think about channeling your inner child in your pursuit of the love of your life.

Head to the park, walk barefoot in the grass and ride on the swings. Take every opportunity to kick through leaves in the Fall and don't be above stomping in puddles in the rain.

Yes it's childish, and yes, that's the point. Keeping up a veneer of sophistication can be a chore at times so loosen up now and again. It's a great way to get in touch with who you really are, and you can add all these things to dancing like no one's watching and singing like no one's listening, so that at some point you can love like you've never been hurt. And don't be surprised if you get hit on by an equally free-spirited playmate-to-soulmate as a result.

Think about things you did and enjoyed as a child and revisit them. Go cycling for the sheer pleasure of it. It doesn't have to be a workout or a race, just fun.

Find a café or bar with board games or one that holds games nights and relive the joy of simple pursuits like Jenga or

Monopoly, or have a games night at home with charades or a Wii. You're often fiercely competitive so remember it's not all about winning!

Your sign also has a strong natural affinity with children so spend time with your nieces or nephews, or with your friends' kids as this is another great way to meet your love match that you may not have thought of.

Help out at parties, take younger children to a movie or chaperone them to gigs if they're a little older. In fact do anything to give their parents a break. A good word from a child who thinks you're pretty cool can kindle interest in you from their good-looking single uncle, or their father's unattached friends who may also be on call to help out with occasional child care. Baby-sitting suddenly becomes a whole new and much more romantic way to spend an evening when you have a handsome hunk on hand to help you out. And single dads would adore a woman who really gets on with their children too, so you're already opening up your romantic options if you're happy to take on a ready-made family.

A trip to the zoo, with or without children in tow, especially to see the lions, could be a particularly good place for you to meet your love match. Check your best love times before you go and put your animal magnetism to work to draw some romance into your life.

3. Get Some Sunshine

As a Fire sign you're often at your best when the heat is on. As an Aries, you also tend to push yourself to the limits when it comes to work so if planning a vacation keeps slipping to last place on your to-do list raise it to top priority right now and allow yourself some downtime to follow the sun. If you work hard, you've a right to play hard too.

July and August tend to be when you're at your hottest romantically as Venus, planet of love, is usually in your sign during these months. This makes you even more attractive to potential partners.

If your ruler Mars happens to be in your sign too (check the dates in the 'Venus and Mars' chapter to find out) you're practically guaranteed to meet someone special.

If you're really serious about finding 'the one' and can book your breaks away to coincide with when the planets are on your side you're really helping your cause, but taking a vacation anywhere at any time will enhance your chances when it comes to finding love.

And the more playfulness you exude while you're away from your usual environment, the better. If you want to play beach volleyball go for it, otherwise do something creative like making a sand sculpture or building an amazing sandcastle. These options tap into getting in touch with your inner child too, so you have a double whammy of increasing your powers of attraction.

The key is to get yourself noticed in a good way by being active. Lounging on the beach all day will get you nothing but sunburned. (And if a beach holiday isn't your style, going on safari is particularly well-starred for you in your search for love.)

So connect, explore the location or resort you're in, try out different places to eat, and mix and mingle. You could click with a hotel entertainer or musician, a holiday representative, or someone you meet when you're out dancing at a place with a party atmosphere. It could be with a guy selling jewelry on the beach, or with a charismatic hotel manager or flamboyant restaurant owner.

The key thing is that the more people you meet while you're away, the more likely you are to hit it off with someone special. This may sound obvious but as an added incentive, yours is one of the signs most likely to enjoy a holiday romance that could turn into something that lasts forever. And it doesn't mean you'll have to move abroad to be with him as he's just as likely to be someone from your own country who has similar tastes in vacation destinations, so that's a good sign in itself.

What better reason do you need to find your passport and get packing?

4. Get Lucky

Love is a lottery, a game of chance. You've just increased your odds of winning by using this book to help you to be in the right place at the right time to meet your Mr. Right.

But there's also a special connection for your sign with romance and with taking the odd calculated risk. So when you're looking for love, you could think about having a day at the races, a night at the casino, living it up in Las Vegas or even playing the arcade games at the end of the pier at the beach.

This could be a way of helping you to bet on a sure thing when it comes to finding the man of your dreams. Just remember that you don't have to spend huge amounts of money in order to get lucky, though if you do happen to win the love jackpot in Vegas you can take your pick of wedding chapels to tie the knot.

Making connections in all the right places is the name of this game. It could be the croupier at the blackjack table who winds up winning your heart, or you could be a would-be millionaire's lucky charm at the roulette wheel and end up together forever.

But since it's the location that's the key thing, you could meet your match far from the gaming tables and slot machines at a café at a casino complex or at an on-site cabaret show.

The connection for love doesn't have to be anything grand. It might be as simple as winning the prize at the tombola stall at a fund-raising day at your old school, and connecting with a nice guy who's helping on the stall, or with a gorgeous children's entertainer while you're there.

Anything connected to games is good for you romantically too, because while there's no gambling involved it does entail a risk as the aim is to win. So you might encounter your future love at a bowling night, a paint-balling day out or at a local or major sporting event.

And if you're against sporting events where animals are used there could still be the promise of love. You could meet someone who feels exactly the same way as you who turns out to be your soulmate, so you hook up together to run a rescue center for greyhounds, and live happily ever after.

The possibilities are out there but they're not always obvious, so look for connections no matter how bizarre they might seem at first, and your prize could be a trophy boyfriend.

5. Get Planning a Party

Your sign has a higher chance than other signs of hooking up with a long-term partner at any kind of party.

Wedding receptions are superb places for you to meet the man of your dreams, as loved-up brides are often keen to match-make their friends so you may have been seated next to someone gorgeous and single on purpose. Lucky you.

The romance of the situation often puts the idea of long-term love into the hearts and minds of single guests, so work that in your favor and say yes to any and all invitations to weddings that come your way.

If friends just aren't getting hitched so invitations are scarce, be enterprising and involve yourself in other people's weddings in a creative way. Ideally this has to be something that puts you on show, not behind the scenes washing dishes, though the stars may conspire for you to meet your soulmate who could be the chef preparing the wedding buffet. Take a part-time job to help out with catering or as waiting staff, or if you're a great photographer offer your services.

Also consider organizing a party of your own. There are so many reasons for a good get-together. Halloween, Christmas, your own birthday party or a friend's, children's parties (which again taps into your inner child option), or just celebrating the fact that it's Tuesday. You're innovative enough to come up with any excuse for a party, and costume parties or 'dressing to impress' themes are particularly well-starred for your sign.

To really help things along tie it in with the dates and times when love is more likely to come your way using the checklists at the back of the book.

These phases would be perfect for a singles party. It could be a barbecue or a pot-luck dinner where everyone brings a course to share, or you could have it at a restaurant to make it easier still.

So that you're meeting quality potential soulmates ask your single friends to bring along a guy they like but who for some reason is just not for them. Not that there's anything wrong with him, he could be a friend's brother that you've never met, or he could be best buddies with your gal pal who just never felt that romantic connection. Why let a good man go to waste when he could be introduced to you and your female friends?

There's every chance that someone who comes to one of your parties will fall for you, and your friends will love you for it as they could strike it lucky too.

You could ring the changes and take turns to host events, but it's going to be 'leader of the pack' you who gets the ball rolling. And if you get really good at it, you'll have added to your talents as a party planner, and doing it professionally could be yet another way of extending your circle to meet the man you're meant to be with. Turning a hobby into a business is something your sign has a real knack for.

6. Get Passionate

What's your passion? Apart from finding Mr. Right, of course. Name the one thing you really love doing that, when you're doing it, absorbs you so completely that you lose all track of time and forget who and where you are.

It could be writing, life drawing, photography, dancing, running, acting. You fill in the blanks. Whatever it is, there's a group or society that loves to do it too, so get connected with people who enjoy what you do and you're a step closer to romance.

And if there isn't a place near you to indulge in your favorite thing, Aries is the sign of the initiator so think about starting one. It's a great way to get yourself known and to communicate with more people, and the more people you know, the better, in the quest for romance.

Only you know what it is that floats your boat, but getting creative and making or producing things that are useful or, ideally, beautiful is something that puts you firmly in the right place for finding love. Men who have a creative or artistic streak are really right for you, so you could consider selling anything you might make at a design fair where blacksmiths, woodturners and other macho makers will be. Making things using fire and metal, especially gold, is something your sign could be skilled at too.

You could even find love on a confidence-building course where you get to fire-walk, or while learning circus skills, as someone you meet who excels at fire-eating could also be hot stuff when it comes to kissing. But don't dismiss even the most mundane or unusual interests that give you pleasure. Everything has potential if you look for it.

The main thing is this: If you're happy, you're generating a whole new vibration that is much more alluring for guys to pick up on than someone who's just waiting to be rescued from boredom by some fantasy ideal man. There's a saying: 'When the student is ready the teacher will appear'. Think of it instead as 'When you're ready, the right guy will appear'.

While you're working on finding your passion, consider that one reason you might not have found the love you want so far may be because there's something you need to do or achieve creatively first. Women in particular often put their own passions on hold once they're in a relationship so think hard about whether you'd rather be with someone right now than write that book, or do that art course or... insert your personal passion here.

Remember, this is all about timing, so the right man will be there when you're ready for him. But also remember that you can't procrastinate forever, so use the fiery element of your sign to make things happen.

7. Get Regal

While looking for your Prince Charming pay special attention to places that have a royal connection.

While the odds of snagging a real life prince may not be high, if only because there aren't enough to go around, the kind of man most suited to you is likely to have a noble bearing and an air of entitlement about him.

He may even have an entourage who hang on his every word and treat him like a king. So it's only natural that you might find him living in a castle or stately home, or at the very least somewhere that has a regal air about it or a royal-sounding name.

Bringing things back down to earth, he could work in a heritage building re-enacting scenes from bygone days, or as a tour guide, or he could just be someone who's fascinated by the grandeur of the past.

The man for you might also be connected to the gold industry, or specialize in selling or making gold jewelry.

Putting it all together from another angle, he could be a party animal who wears gold bling, hangs out at the 'Empire' club, and lists a major royal-sounding burger chain as his favorite place to eat!

That might sound like romantic hell or heaven to you, but take it up a few notches, and you could genuinely meet the man of your dreams at a restaurant or venue with some sort of royal connection or name, 'The King of Siam' Thai restaurant for instance, or bump into him in Princes Street or Kings Walk or...

you get the picture.

And rather than Mr. T-style golden overload, he could wear a signature stunning but tasteful gold designer watch, or a simple piece of personal jewelry, also in gold.

It's all about looking for clues, no matter how subtle, and making sure that you're extra alert on the days when the stars are lining up for love.

If you're traveling far on your best love days, or going on vacation, think about visiting the gold souk in Dubai, or try your hand at panning for gold in California. You could visit the gold mining areas in Australia, or the same country's amazing Gold Coast.

Keep your options open, though it's not vital to travel a long way to meet your soulmate. He could be the guy dressed in a crown and velvet robes at a costume party around the corner from your place. And that could be the beginning of a right royal romance.

Location Checklist

A checklist is a handy way to get you focused and pinpoint those places you might add to your schedule in order to help love along. This is not an exhaustive list by any means but will give you some ideas, and help you think of many more along similar lines. You could meet 'the one' at a:

- Theater club
- Amateur dramatic society
- Playgroup
- Children's party
- Park
- Playground
- Beach
- Kids' movie
- Las Vegas

- Zoo
- Horse racing
- Gold souk
- Wedding reception
- Cycle ride
- Smart restaurant
- Opera
- On vacation
- Costume party

When you've found your perfect partner, you can look back at your checklist and smile at the memory of that time in the park when your nephew's Frisbee flew past you, but was caught by that handsome guy who laughed and joined in the game. He turned out to be an actor who'd just got a break in a Hollywood movie, whisked you out there to join him and you took a gamble and before too long sealed your love in a little chapel in Las Vegas. And the rest is history. Insert your own romantic 'how we met' story instead, of course.

Chapter 2

Where to Find Love if You're Taurus

The rumor on the astrological grapevine is that you're such a sensual creature that by rights you should have a long line of potential lovers already queuing up to make your acquaintance.

If only the road to romance were that easy! While it's true you're likely to have something about you that's attractive, tactile, a little earthy in a good way and kind of comforting too, all of which adds up to a potent and desirable mix for a vast number of guys, you're more picky than perhaps even you realize. You won't settle for just anyone, and while that's no bad thing it could be the reason you haven't yet found Mr. Right.

For you, love is about quality rather than quantity. Although Taurus does have a reputation for overindulgence, that only really kicks in where you've discovered something that's worthy of your attention, makes you feel good and, once hooked, you can't get enough of. That might go for rich, dark chocolate (as your sign often has a sweet tooth) where only the best will do, for classy clothes in sensuous fabrics, and for home furnishings that are so comfortable and soft you just want to stroke and nestle into them.

It makes sense that this should apply to your partner too. Rich, classy and sensuous? Tick, tick and tick.

Once you know what you like and you get it, you do tend to stick with it. In a relationship you're someone who's in it for the long haul, and you hate to play games as you can be incredibly possessive. What's yours is yours, and that goes for people too. Any hint of instability or, worse, infidelity can turn you into a green-eyed raging bull.

So the man for you is someone who not only shares your love of good things, but who appreciates your sense of loyalty and admires your determination and perseverance.

He also encourages you to be the best you can possibly be, because he wants to be proud of you. So he may tend to prod you into action now and again, possibly slightly out of your comfort zone, to achieve the high standards you both adore.

This could mean encouraging you to take more care of your health and fitness, something the man for you is likely to be particularly vigilant about. But love is a two-way thing so while you may heed his advice and exercise more, he'll also benefit from tuning in to your more laid-back take on life, which is to sometimes sit back and smell the roses.

I can personally vouch for these next tips working. I'm a Taurus who hates going to the gym, but it's where I met a long-term love who happened to be the head of a local recycling company. He was the fittest man I'd ever met, immaculate in the way he looked after his appearance and cleaned the house (he'd turn vacuuming the rugs into a sweat-inducing workout!), and was an excellent cook. So that ticked five boxes.

If you meet a man in any of the following locations who fits just one of these categories, as you should, you're onto a winner.

1. Get Healing

In the search for love, combining what you enjoy doing with learning a new skill puts you as a Taurus in a better position to meet the right kind of man.

So learning an alternative therapy would be a wonderful use of your sign's naturally heightened senses. Aromatherapy and massage are areas you have a real affinity with. You're so sensually aware that you almost know instinctively where to place your hands to soothe either your own or someone else's pain. You're also particularly tuned in to the power of natural plant-based scents and aromas, so selecting oils to enhance a mood or overcome ailments could be an ideal occupation or part-time interest for you.

You have an innate understanding of how emotional distress links with physical pain, and with guidance, could become a gifted therapist and healer using your natural talents.

How might this help you meet a potential partner? He could be your tutor or a fellow student, or someone you meet while buying the equipment or oils you need at a health store. And as massage and aromatherapy are also treatments that would benefit you, you might encounter your future love in another therapist's clinic where you're both waiting for your appointments.

Nutrition is another area that would be ideal for your sign. If you're a true Taurus food is one of your passions, but along with that passion can sometimes come weight issues. So use your fascination for food to study it and understand it, and make it work for you, not only in terms of your own health and career prospects but also for your romantic future.

Again, you could hook up with someone who teaches you, or a guy you meet on a course, or a volunteer who you practice your evolving skills on could turn out to have a very healing effect on your love life.

Weight loss and dieting groups also hold potential for you to meet Mr. Right. Aiming to get slimmer, fitter and healthier to impress someone you'd like in your life is one of the key incentives for improving body image. It's not about being skinny, it's about being healthy. And it's not about being someone you're not, it's about being able to make the most of life rather than being held back by health concerns or lack of confidence if you don't feel you look your best.

It's not essential to study in depth and make healing your profession in order to find love, but taking an interest, especially in alternative health ideas, could put you on the right path. Mind, Body and Spirit fairs or health conventions could be among the kinds of places to meet your soulmate. It just takes a little thought to put yourself in the right place at the right time to meet the right guy.

2. Get Informed

You don't have to be a genius to attract a worthwhile mate, but some smart moves on your part could certainly help you to push things in the right direction.

There's a strong chance that the man of your dreams is a particularly bright guy so to find him you need to go to the kind of places he's more likely to hang out.

The library is a good start, and if you haven't been to one for a while they're now a far cry from the silent halls of knowledge they used to be. Expect to find internet zones, magazines and DVDs to browse through if you don't fancy yourself as an intellectual type, or even if you do.

While you're there you could look up new things to do in your local area, find information about joining a group that appeals to you, or become a member of the book club. Add these to your 'where to find love' locations list below, but also think about connecting with guys you encounter during your visit.

As an Earth sign, you'll appreciate that things, including love, don't always come instantly and it's by putting in some work that you'll get results. So make your trips a frequent thing, since it's much easier to bond with someone if you do something on a regular basis as your face becomes more familiar than to expect an immediately attraction and to be swept off your feet. Try to tie visits in with your best astrological love dates to help things along even more.

Think about spending time in your local bookstores too, especially ones that have coffee shops attached so you can browse through books and cast an eye over other browsers as well. And don't be too shy to ask that cute guy on the help desk for recommendations. You could come away with a new man and a whole new fiction genre to explore together.

If the library or bookstore is not your thing then a pub or bar quiz could be just the place. Show off your specialist knowledge or your head for trivia and get together with a team that makes the whole thing a lot of fun. The kind of guy who's a good fit for you is a walking treasure-trove of useful and accurate information, and he'll be impressed if you can answer a few questions that he can't.

The key for romantic success here is to seek out places where you can find men who know their stuff. Your ideal match could be at an advice bureau, on a call center helpline, or a tourist information office. And the best thing of all is that you'll have a perfect reason to talk to him by asking for information, so no worries about making the first move or breaking the ice.

3. Get Physical

The kind of man who does it for you, let's be honest, is one who's easy on the eye. That could be said for pretty much everyone, but as you're ruled by Venus beauty appeals to your sign more than most.

You need to be surrounded by things (and in an ideal world, people) who are pleasing to the senses in every way, so a great place for you to meet a vision of physical perfection could be at the gym. Where else will you find men who like to take care of their bodies, partly for their own pleasure but mostly to attract the likes of you?

The potentially tricky thing here is that you'll have to become a gym bunny too, which may or may not be your style. But what have you got to lose? Maybe a few pounds if you need to, and think of the boost that will give you. If you feel more attractive you radiate confidence.

And if treadmills, weights and aerobics don't appeal, think about trying more serene classes, as your nature tends to draw you to the kind of exercise where you get to lie down occasionally. Yoga and Pilates, though still strenuous and effective, fit that bill perfectly and attract a more thoughtful kind of man too. Pilates especially helps him to look good and toned, but he likes to engage his mind as well as his muscles when he works out and that combination, for you, is a potent romantic mix.

Or you could join a walking group as it's one of the best forms of exercise you can get, and you can do it at your own pace which is ideal as Taureans tend to thrive when they can do things their own sweet way. And as this is meant to be about pleasure too, why hurry? It also puts you in the natural environment for your sign, the great outdoors, plus it gets you in the company of countryside-loving men who are likely to be on the right side of fit.

The point about pleasure and leisure is key for you, in life as well as when it comes to finding love. You don't have to become a fitness junkie to find your other half, but fitness of sorts is a connection you should look out for, no matter how tenuous it might seem. And remember that it's the timing that counts too.

So on the days your stars align for love you could find yourself browsing for designer trainers at a cool shoe store, or watching a local cycle race, or even cheering on your children (if you have any) at a school sports day when the man of your dreams catches your eye. In fact a sports teacher or coach could be a match made in the heavens for you.

The link with getting physical, active and healthier will be obvious if you stay alert so you don't miss an opportunity to connect.

4. Get Cooking

Whether you're typical of your sign and love food or simply see food as fuel, there's good reason to hone your culinary skills on the path to love.

There's something undeniably sexy about a man who can throw a decent meal together without getting flustered, and as more men are turning their hands to making fancy food, where better to find the missing ingredient to your romantic life than on a cookery course?

The more specialized the course, the more likely you are to find the kind of man to your taste, though if you truly do need to go back to basics, you can still be sure of some male company while you both learn to cook up a storm.

Vegetarian meals, cooking for a special diet or to improve a specific health issue are the kinds of courses where you're most likely to meet the man who's right for you.

You'll get to share conversation, tips and techniques then share what you've baked or broiled together at the end of each session. And there's very little that's more romantic, or erotic, than feeding each other a taste of the delicacies you've prepared.

Again, think of this as not just an exercise to get yourself a man but as a way to expand your world, your interests and your talents too.

Other ways to link with this are where you buy your food. Look for organic, free range and healthy options when you shop and you're almost bound to bump into the kind of guy who could rock your romantic world. You're more likely to find him selling his own artisan bread or offering earthy, organic vegetables for sale at a farmer's market, or delivering your organic veggie box. But you could also find him serving at the deli counter at your local supermarket, or shopping there for unusual ingredients for some home-cooked specialty, so choose your aisles wisely if you want to some day share a shopping trolley with him.

You might meet him over a meal at a vegetarian restaurant with communal seating. The guy for you generally doesn't do fast food and is quite a stickler when it comes to hygiene, so venues that are crisp, white, scrubbed and clean-looking are more his kind of hangout. It doesn't have to be a classy restaurant but it does have to be spotless with great tasting, simple and fresh food.

He might even work there or own the place, so you could potentially win his heart by becoming one of his best customers.

Dinner dating agencies are another option to explore, as your sign is extra likely to bond with someone special over a delicious meal that appeals to all your senses.

So look for a man who knows and loves good food, and if the timing is right you can't go wrong.

5. Get Recycling

The natural environment is likely to be very important to you, as Earth signs thrive on being close to nature, so your ideal man may be connected to preserving the world around you and looking to safeguard it for future generations.

He might be an eco warrior, working for Greenpeace, a campaigner trying to get support to save a local area of natural beauty, or the guy you see every Sunday when you take your cardboard boxes and plastic bottles to the recycling center.

He could work for a firm that prints on recycled paper, so you could encounter him trying to persuade you or your company to go for a greener option with letterheads and business cards.

The man for you is very good with his hands and creative too, but almost always in a practical way. Because he's into recycling he could be someone who's building or renovating his home using reclaimed materials. Or if he's creating things from reclaimed wood they'll be useful items: Chairs, tables or wooden containers rather than anything too frivolous. And with your excellent if rather expensive taste you could meet him at a craft or design fair where he's selling his fabulous one-off pieces, though he's just as likely to be someone who enjoys making simpler, more basic items for his own use from his garden shed. They'll still be beautifully finished and he'll still have exactly the right tools for the job though, as he considers himself a craftsman.

Another way to get together with him is to join a local environmental group to help raise green awareness in your community. He's likely to be a key player, making things happen rather than just discussing grandiose theories. You'll recognize him by his neat appearance, clear thinking and the precise and convincing way he puts his points across.

Issues connected to genetically modified food, local health or education services are the kinds of things to get him all fired up. Or he might be involved in local wildlife conservation. While not exactly connected to recycling, all of these do involve preserving natural resources and keeping local communities healthy, happy and in employment.

Your contribution in a situation like this could be that once you get motivated to support a cause there's no stopping you until you get results, as perseverance is one of your sign's major strengths. So joining forces with this guy to make the world a better place could make you a power couple in the best possible way.

6. Get Clean

It's a Taurus trait to want to look your best (more often than not), and the things you wear are usually good quality and made to last. You might have a few cheap and cheerful items in your wardrobe to update your look, but if you're true to type you'd rather have cotton, silk or wool next to your skin rather than synthetics.

Natural fibers last, but at a price, so you'll need to keep your prized possessions pristine by regular cleaning and mending.

Believe it or not, the dry cleaners, shoe repairers and alterations services of the world are superb places for you to meet your love match. It could be someone working there, but it's just as likely to be one of their other customers who looks after his possessions with as much care as you do. Check your best times for love and one of the most important romantic days of your life could be the day you take your coat in for dry cleaning. It doesn't matter that you don't meet in a glamorous situation, the point is that you meet.

The same goes for your home. If you need to call in professional cleaners to spruce up the carpets, you could be opening the front door to your future partner.

If the washing machine breaks down you may be praising rather than cursing the day, as destiny could bring you a love interest in the shape of the repair man, or it could result in you meeting your future partner in the local laundromat.

And if you have a garden that needs to be tidied up and organized, call in an expert and you could find that romance blossoms as a result. Someone specializing in planting herb gardens and medicinal plants in particular could have a real affinity with you, and if he suggests that you need a vegetable patch consider it a clear sign that he's got real soulmate potential, as this doubles your love chances by tying in with your 'Get Cooking' option.

The man for you is extremely practical and highly efficient, possibly obsessively so, so exchanging some of his finicky ways for a few of your equally thorough but more relaxed ideas on getting things done will help to build a balanced relationship that can go the distance.

Undoubtedly, this sounds a little crazy, but astrology is about symbolism as well as good timing, so trust the stars to bring you the clean sweep your love life needs.

7. Get a Pet

While it's clearly just plain wrong to have a pet as a fashion accessory to fit into your Louis Vuitton handbag, it's no bad thing to have an endearing furry friend to help you win in the love stakes.

Owning a pet of any sort, but particularly for you one that's soft to stroke because of your tactile ways, is an excellent option for your sign because so long as you don't have allergies having a pet in your life can be good for your health.

Something to love, pamper, care for and play with can make you feel needed and wanted, and gives you a focus for sharing affection as you have a lot of love to give. But having a pet can also help you find that (so far) elusive man.

A dog is a great icebreaker, as a cute pooch is an instant topic of conversation. And walking your dog, or someone else's, is a great way to connect to new people and get to know them better without feeling obliged to take things further. You may find you like their dog but realize that you're not so keen on them. A dog in particular helps keep you fit, which connects nicely with your 'Get Physical' option too.

If you can't have a pet of your own, try volunteering at an animal sanctuary. It's emotionally fulfilling as you'd be helping a bunch of loveless waifs and strays, and it's the kind of thing that good-hearted guys tend to get involved with so you know you'll be meeting men who are in touch with their sensitive and caring side, at least when it comes to animals.

You could always take this a step further and become a professional dog walker or pet sitter, and get to know someone romantically through your work.

Pet shows, talent contests and animal agility competitions are also good ways to put meeting your romantic match high on your agenda. You might encounter a man with a working dog, perhaps a farmer whose canine companion rounds up sheep, or a police dog handler whose super bright mutt wins awards for its speed and for sniffing out trouble.

A man who owns animals himself could also be the one for you. Wherever you meet him, it's worth asking him if he has any pets as again this is a good sign that you're on the same romantic wavelength.

And don't forget that a trip to the veterinary surgery could also see you paired up with your perfect partner. You could meet him while you're in the waiting room, or maybe you'll fall for the veterinarian himself.

Location Checklist

A checklist is a handy way to get focused and pinpoint those places you need to add to your routine in order to help love along. This is not an exhaustive list by any means but will give you some ideas, and help you think of many more along similar lines. You could meet 'the one' at a:

- Health food store
- Alternative therapy center
- Cookery course
- Smart delicatessen
- Doctor's surgery
- Library
- Bookstore
- Gym
- Pub quiz
- Yoga class
- Recycling center
- Veterinary surgery
- Dog walking
- Laundromat
- Dry cleaners
- Tailoring or alteration service
- Vegetarian restaurant
- Pet rescue center

When you've found your perfect partner, you can look back at your checklist and smile at the memory of that time at the yoga class when the gorgeous tutor helped to ease you into a particularly challenging pose. When you bumped into him later while out walking your friend's dog, he invited you to join him for dinner at a fabulously romantic organic restaurant in the countryside. And the rest is history. Insert your own romantic 'how we met' story instead, of course.

Chapter 3

Where to Find Love if You're Gemini

'So many men, so little time' could be your sign's mantra. It's not just about quantity for you but as a Gemini it is about sampling what's out there before making a choice and sticking with it.

This can be the hardest thing ever for you as there's always the possibility that something or someone more interesting might be just around the corner.

Your ideal mate should be cool, or he should be practical, or rich, or handsome, or all of these things, or none of them. And so on until you drive yourself crazy as you change your mind from day to day or sometimes from hour to hour.

If you admit it, you'll see that part of you is scared of making the wrong decision, so your new priority on the road to successful and long-term romance is to work out what you really want from a relationship and what you're prepared to give in return.

You're unlikely to be short of admirers because you're stimulating, exciting, unpredictable and great fun to be with, and dating you is twice the fun as it's like dating two people.

The potential downside of this is that others are never quite sure where they stand with you, as once you've found a guy you like you can be equally fickle, on again, off again as the mood takes you.

Sometimes you probably wonder if this whole relationship thing is really for you as it seems the moment you're close to commitment you do another of your mental backflips and head off to where you think the grass is greener. It's a true 'Runaway Bride' moment, but it doesn't have to be that way.

Out there is someone who can play you at your own game, and you do love to play games and match wits with potential partners. You also love to talk, so someone who loves to listen is clearly going to be a winner. And if he can keep you fascinated and mentally stimulated in return he'll have found the key to your heart.

Until now, you've most likely been attracted to guys who may be larger than life and a little overwhelming. Fascinating, informative and funny they may be, but they'll also overlook the subtle details in life that you adore, and may be just a little too outdoorsy and outgoing to make you truly happy. While you're undeniably sociable you prefer to be intimately acquainted with where you are and what's around you, with those people and places that are a bus ride away at most.

The one area you do seem to agree on with your usual type is no strings, no commitments, but that may be wearing thin for you now. Because as a Gemini, you more than other signs (but along with fellow air sign Libra) are looking for your other half to complete you. Your sign is symbolized by twins showing your dual nature, the yin and yang, masculine and feminine side, though you may not be aware of it.

As a result of this, while you might have a picture in your head of a manly, athletic type as your ideal match you may in fact be more drawn to men who are in touch with their feminine side. If he can cook and clean house as well as listen to you, enjoy stimulating conversations and look amazing (which with your ideal match is more than likely), what's not to love?

All you have to do, of course, is find him. If until now you've been looking for love in all the wrong places here's your astrological map to help you find your perfect partner.

1. Get Wordy

Words are what make you tick. You love to talk, read, research, explore, investigate, discuss, debate and yes, at times gossip. You have to know exactly what's going on at work, in your neighborhood and on your favorite TV shows.

And luckily for you the man who would suit you best enjoys the art of conversation too. Better still, he's likely to be a good listener because sometimes when you start talking you're hard to stop!

So you're blessed with an abundance of places to find your perfect man. He could be on a creative writing course, so as you also love words and the chance to learn something new you could think about signing up for a writing course too. He's a romantic sort so a class that focuses on poetry might give you more of a chance to hook up with him.

And if you know nothing about poetry you could begin to hang out at poetry festivals, open-mic nights or poetry slams in bars or cafés where writers stand up and read their work. This may not be something you'd normally consider doing but it's all part of expanding your experience and social networks so it's worth a try. You don't even have to participate, just listen, as it's being in the right place at the right time that's going to make a difference to your love life.

Look out also for events where you get to talk and share ideas. It could be at a book club discussing favorite novels, a talk on well-being at a health store open night, or hooking up with a group that gets neighbors and communities together to discuss local issues. Keeping things close to home is more beneficial for you when it comes to finding love, and events at nearby schools or educational centers or spaces used for counseling or legal matters of any kind are key locations for you to meet your match.

You can't get any closer to home than networking via your computer. This is absolutely made for your sign. You could start a blog about something that's important to you. It could be anything at all, so long as you make it fascinating and preferably funny.

You're the expert at the quick one-liner and the witty comment, so Twitter is ideal for you. You get to follow people who are on your wavelength and with luck they'll follow you right back. And communities and camaraderie build up surprisingly quickly considering you're conversing with people you've most probably never met.

Online dating is great for you too as being able to connect with someone on the internet before you meet him helps you get to know him before making any kind of commitment. You love words but you're also adept at reading between the lines so you can weed out the hopefuls from the hopeless. The way to your heart is through your mind so finding someone who woos you with eloquent emails means that by the time you do meet up the chances are you'll already be a little in love.

2. Get Musical

Look out for the man of your dreams at music events, especially any in your neighborhood that may be in intimate, candle-lit venues. It's all about setting the mood for romance, and the man for you thrives in harmonious surroundings which are conducive to the gentle art of seduction as well as the art of conversation.

You're more likely to encounter Mr. Right at small-scale jazz, blues, rock or classical music events than at a gig by your favorite boy band so select your music and your venue wisely. Clearly you need to take your own listening taste into consideration but your sign's ability to embrace new experiences should enable you to open up to different musical experiences with ease.

An acoustic duo in a café would be perfect. There's a subliminal message being sent by being in the presence of duos, especially a boy-girl combination if you're a gal seeking a guy. It reinforces the idea that two is better than one.

It's also never too late to start music lessons. Even if you only play for your own pleasure it's a skill worth having, and who knows who you might meet at a practice session, music lesson or impromptu jam if you feel confident enough and get good enough at your chosen instrument.

Two is your magic number so if you do choose to go down this route learning one-on-one is better than a group session. A friend of a friend could put you in touch with the perfect teacher who could turn out to be your perfect life partner.

Vocal harmony is great for you too and for the man you're well suited to being with. You love to be heard so that could extend to singing, and the man for you is likely to have a delicious voice that's worth listening to. So if you can sing or would like to, explore the possibility of joining forces with a gorgeous guy to make beautiful musical duets with.

One of the best ways of all to meet your match with a musical soundtrack is to go dancing, or better still to go to a dance class. Learning something for pleasure is a recurring theme in your quest for romance. Make sure it's the kind of dancing where you get to partner up and make some serious moves together. Salsa and close up dances like the rumba where you're 'in hold' rather than dancing apart could really help those romantic sparks ignite.

3. Get Legal

Your sign loves to know what's going in the world around you, and your instinct for information often means that you're first person to find out and reveal the hot news of the day. This could be connected to the latest celebrity gossip that you share with friends, important news at work, or what's going on in your neighborhood or with your siblings if you have them.

But when it comes to romance, you'll be in your element where news is being made at your local law court, as well as in the right place to encounter potential partners.

It may sound bizarre but because you have the kind of mind that thrives on puzzles and solving mysteries, and your sign often loves working out 'whodunnit' in crime-based TV dramas, movies or novels, this is just about taking your fascination for those scenarios a step further.

Even if that isn't your kind of thing, stretching yourself to develop even a passing interest in your local legal proceedings is a good thing to do, as it takes you out of your usual routine and opens up a whole new world where you might find love.

Ideally you'll be in court as a spectator and not as a participant and, fingers crossed, you'll end up with a lawyer rather than someone about to be sentenced.

Barristers, solicitors and judges all have strong romantic potential for you, as do guys with any connection to the legal profession. You could even find you have a romantic encounter with a traffic cop or the person you need to pay your parking fine to, though it's obviously not worth racking up fines or getting into trouble just to find a partner.

If men in uniform float your boat you could try a uniform dating site. Men in any kind of law enforcement role could be just right for you. And although not directly linked to the legal profession (although he might be) someone in the Air Force could rock your world. As an Air sign, this elemental connection is surprisingly strong for you when contemplating a partnership.

Alternatively you could fall for someone who provides free or low cost legal advice, or meet your match at the signing of the marriage certificate at a friend's wedding in a registrar's office. Weddings are almost always a great way to hook up with single, available guys, especially for your sign where there's that subliminal message about being part of a couple working its magic all over again.

But it's not just about the legal system or its professions, it's also about the location. Check your best love days and if you're somewhere that has a link with the law at the times highlighted for you, that's where and when you could find you're likely to be sentenced to a lifetime of love.

4. Get Beautiful

It goes without saying that you're beautiful already, but places you may go to get even more gorgeous could provide a higher than average chance of you finding your future partner.

You might think it's unlikely that a beauty spa is a good hunting ground for a mate but think again. Many are owned by men, and often treatments are provided for guys too so you could strike it lucky with the hottie sharing the Jacuzzi with you.

Hairdressing salons are also great places to meet a potential soulmate. He could be the cute guy waiting next to you for a haircut or he could be the even cuter guy cutting and styling your hair. As a rule, people in this profession love to talk so you'll have an instant audience with someone who has natural charm and an easy rapport, and there'll be no danger of the thing you hate most, awkward silences.

Alternatively, you could hit it off with a dermatologist or skin specialist. Both you and the likely object of your affection tend to look younger than your years (it's an Air sign thing). So investing in treatments, or getting advice on creams or facials to prolong that look is another way of meeting someone on your romantic wavelength too.

And if tattoos are your idea of beauty you could even meet your match at your local tattoo parlor, as the man for you may have major artistic skills. Just make sure he really is your forever guy before he inks his name in a permanent love heart on your skin.

It's not just about the body beautiful either. Places you go to buy beautiful things to adorn yourself with are equally lucky for your love life.

You might bump into your future partner while admiring precious gems in a jewelry store window, though you're more likely to have a close encounter with a desirable customer or the jeweler himself if you go in to get a new battery for your watch, or have a favorite necklace repaired.

A stylish adviser in a fashion store could turn out to be the one for you, or you might find that asking a random bystander's opinion on something you're about to purchase could lead to romance. Or ask him where he got that great tie, shirt, T-shirt, whatever and you could get the same result. The man for you particularly appreciates others noticing the efforts he's gone to in order to look good, but in a subtle, tasteful, low key way.

Again it's about thinking laterally rather than literally, and keeping your radar on so that you're in the right place at the right time. Offer your services at a charity fashion show and you could be strutting the catwalk with your future Mr. Right. It'd be a unique way to see how you'd fit together walking down the aisle.

5. Get (And Give) Information

Because you're so curious about what's going on around you and why, you tend to know a little about a lot and have information at your fingertips. You're the go-to gal for everything from bus timetables to obscure trivia, so one way to connect with your future Significant Other, who also likes to be well-informed, is to be in places where people get or give information.

You could meet him at an advice center or travel information desk. Either way, your encyclopedic knowledge could help him out of a tricky situation. Or it might be the other way around.

Because he's the ultimate diplomat he might be the public face of a complaints department in a store, so no matter how upset you may because your new purchase doesn't work, he'll send you away with your problem resolved and a smile, and possibly his phone number too.

You could meet him at a music quiz night (so this ties in with your 'Get Musical' option as well) where he's either got all the answers or he's the one who makes the decisions in the event of a tie.

More seriously, you might encounter him on a course in life coaching or counseling as he's the kind of guy who seems to be able to see both sides of any situation and provide a solution that keeps the peace for all concerned.

Think also about situations where mediation is required. If

you're in need of arbitration connected to your career or a dispute with a neighbor he could be your man, in more ways than one.

One Gemini I know even fell for her counselor in couples counseling. While this is not recommended as a means to finding Mr. Right she certainly seemed happier with her new man than she was before, and it shows that someone who listens non-judgmentally and helps you reach your own decisions is very compatible with your sign.

On safer ground, you could meet your future love at the library, while studying or maybe he's working there and helping you out with your own research and quest for information.

Or he could be at a recruitment agency assisting you to find work, or even at a dating agency pairing you up with a soulmate, as the kind of guy for you is skilled at matchmaking people with the right job or with potential partners. Only this time your perfect match could be him.

6. Get Mirroring

Geminis are incredibly adaptable. The chances are you're a great mimic thanks to your sign's symbol, the Twins, so you're able to mirror things back at people often without them realizing it. Maybe you don't even realize you're doing it yourself, as you easily pick up other people's mannerisms, accents and sometimes even the way they think.

What this boils down to is a kind of natural NLP, neuro-linguistic programming, meaning you're able to talk, move and use behavior that reflects and harmonizes with the people you're connecting with. In fact an NLP course could be a great place to find your ideal man as it's the kind of thing that would fascinate him too.

So on the basis that like attracts like, and if you want to increase your chances of drawing the right kind of man to you, you may want to adapt and adopt some of his ways.

How can you do this when you haven't met him yet? Astrologically speaking, you can be sure he likes beautiful things, soft words, serene atmospheres, candlelight and sensual music. So choosing to spend more time in places with that kind of feel will automatically put you more in tune with him. And you increase your chances of finding him there as this is all about being in the right location at the right time too.

He also likes the sweet things in life, so you could meet him in a smart patisserie as he's likely to have a sweet tooth but a slim figure because he looks after himself. Though you could also bump into him buying candy in a convenience store.

Aesthetically pleasing surroundings are highly important to your future love and he's almost sure to have good taste in home design. So you could find that he owns or manages a smart florist's shop or interiors store, possibly specializing in super-cool lighting, chandeliers or even mirrors. If not then you could run into him shopping in these kinds of establishments. Minimalist surroundings are his thing, he doesn't like fuss or clutter, so even a certain Scandinavian homewares superstore may be among his favorite hang outs.

Bear in mind that this isn't about stalking, or being someone you're not in order to hook up with someone fabulous who you might feel is possibly out of your league. Once you're a couple you will, to some degree, merge and take on facets of each other's personalities anyway as your dual-natured signs are both seeking a Significant Other to complete you. So mirroring gives you a chance to try on his lifestyle for size beforehand to see if it suits you. And because you and the man you're meant to be with are a match made in the stars, it's practically guaranteed that it will.

7. Get Arty

If you feel like you've spent a lifetime falling for men that just don't get you, then maybe it's because you're partly denying some of your own needs that haven't been met by the guys you've been out with so far.

No matter who you are or what you do, as a Gemini you love to keep mentally alert and on the move, but there's also a need to balance that with calm and tranquility in your life so try your best to find it. It will soothe your soul and anchor your grasshopper mind.

One way to achieve this is through art, whether you choose to take it up as a skill, which is a great way to meet creative men, or as an art lover attending gallery previews and openings. Keep it local too as somewhere near you is a gallery that needs your support.

You don't have to be knowledgeable about art. Knowing what you like is fine, and a good gallery owner will take the time to explain some of the techniques and meanings of the work you're looking at if you desire that information. Get connected and on the mailing list or join up on social network pages and you'll be invited along to private views where, once the wine starts flowing, conversation will too. You could fall for an artist, an art lover or the gallery owner himself.

You might not consider yourself artistic but your ruling planet Mercury suggests that you're good with your hands, it's just a matter of finding the right thing to keep them occupied.

Words are your strength so you could try a class in calligraphy (writing with a quill or special pen), or making handmade paper, or jewelry inscribed with words. Or you could create amazingly inventive kites which would be perfect for your sign, ruled as it is by air. Even a computer course where you learn to 'airbrush' photographic images to enhance them could work for you, and help you to find love.

It might even be your future Mr. Right who creates air-inspired objects you'll admire, so again look for the clues, whether he makes silver feather necklaces, or is a glass blower or a creator of custom-made woodwind instruments or wind chimes.

You could also look for airy elements in art to put you in the right place to meet your future love. An exhibition of aerial photos, paintings of windmills or birds in flight all have possibilities, or romance could happen for you at an art event held in a former aerodrome.

Adjust this to your own tastes and interests, and remember that the key is hooking up with a guy who appreciates creativity, especially yours.

Location Checklist

A checklist is a handy way to get you focused and pinpoint those places you need to add to your schedule in order to help love along. This is not an exhaustive list by any means but will give you some ideas, and help you think of many more along similar lines. You could meet 'the one' at a:

- Poetry slam
- Art gallery
- Hairdressers
- Beauty salon
- Flower shop
- Jewelry store
- Courtroom
- Music venue
- Jazz club
- Counseling course
- Windmill
- Legal advice center
- Patisserie
- Kite flying tournament
- Internet dating
- Police department
- Dermatology center
- Spa

When you've found your perfect partner, you can look back at your checklist and smile at the memory of that Christmas when your handsome hair stylist took the chance to kiss you under the mistletoe at the salon. You carried on the connection over coffee and cake at a swish patisserie, and it wasn't long before you were picking out a diamond ring together. And the rest is history. Insert your own romantic 'how we met' story instead, of course.

Chapter 4

Where to Find Love if You're Cancer

Home-loving, cake-baking Cancer, you could run up a stylish dress out of old curtains if you had to. You're the quintessential earth mother and, whether you have children or not, people look to you to be nurtured and cared for. At least this is what everyone assumes when they hear what your Sun sign is.

But there's so much more to you than that, and in matters of romance you actually have quite a dark and daring side if you cared to admit it.

Yes, you do rather like the whole caring, sharing thing and you excel at it but you're by no means dull, prim or homely. And underneath that shell you sometimes use to keep people out lurks a heart that likes a little danger, not to mention more than a hint of sensuality.

If, in the past, you've felt that you should play a secondary role in your relationships, to be supportive and nurturing, it's possible that you've done so but felt like you'd lost your own identity in the process. You're looking for a soulmate, and while you may want or even already have children, the last thing you need is a grown man who just wants you to look after his every need without considering yours. Find a man who makes you feel like what you are, a desirable woman, and you could have a match that has the qualities you want to make love stand the test of time.

So when you're looking for romance consider exploring that edgier element of your nature and take a walk on the wild side. This could be the ingredient that's been missing when it comes to finding someone who brings you alive rather than confines you to the sensible, stable but rather safe options others seem to think you should settle for.

It's not about having one-night stands, that's not really your thing. In fact, get it right this time around and your Mr. Right will be the kind of guy who'll always be there for you, come what may. And while you like to feel secure in a relationship, there's a big difference between constancy and complacency.

So it's about being on the same emotional wavelength because you're often ruled by your intuition and your moods. You'd thrive with someone who understands your need for privacy at times, but who also totally gets your desire to feel consumed by passion at others. If he's alert to why you're often a slave to your emotions and your instinct both to protect and worry, then this guy's a keeper who's been worth the wait.

But if you want to make the magic happen you need to take a risk and step out of your comfort zone. Like breaking in a fabulous new pair of shoes, this may hurt at first but once you get used to the idea and the sexy way they make you sashay you wouldn't want things any other way.

So come out of your shell, take a look around, and take a look at yourself too. No one wants their heart battered and bruised but you're a tougher cookie than you think you are.

And what's it to be? Retreat into doing things the way you've always done them, or break the pattern and live life on the edge and to the full for a while? It's worth feeling the fear and doing it anyway if you want to love, and be loved, for life.

1. Get Underground

Your sign's symbol, the crab, sometimes prefers the dark. Just like you. It's quiet, private, healing and a place to think. It's exciting too as it holds the promise of the unexpected, of not knowing what's around the corner.

And while you generally like things to be a bit more regular and routine it's in the darker, unknown reaches of your world that delightfully surprising events can occur when it comes to romance.

So it may sound strange but getting below the surface of everyday life can bring you closer to finding love.

This can be as simple as taking a trip to any big city with an underground transport network and losing yourself in travel. So next time you're journeying by subway, and even more if you commute by underground train on a daily basis, look at the experience and the people around you in a new light. The perfect man for you might have been getting into your carriage at the same time every day for months and you just haven't noticed him. Or he could be the guy who sells you your ticket.

If you're the adventurous type, you could try potholing or spelunking, exploring underground caves. You need to keep your wits about you in the dark, and it's a fact that a little bit of fear heightens all other emotions, so you could bond very closely and very quickly with a fellow adventurer by the time you emerge back into the light.

Being underground doesn't have to be a scary experience, although if you do have a fear of dark and enclosed spaces, it could be at a therapy center to cure your phobia that you meet someone who could become a big part of your world.

Or you could visit a friend who lives in a basement apartment and encounter your perfect man there. If you're thinking about relocating consider basement-living yourself as the love of your life could turn out to be your next-door neighbor.

Visiting a coal mining or diamond mining exhibition or even fossicking for opals in the Australian Outback could help you find love too. It may not seem like your thing but that's not entirely the point. It's being in the right place at the right time that makes the difference. You might meet a miner or a millionaire who's looking for the perfect diamond and his ideal woman to wear it, which could be you.

Also look out for less obvious underground connections. A nightclub named 'Subway' could be where you're meant to meet your dream man, or it could even happen at the fast food chain of the same name.

The stars often give you a nudge in the right direction without you realizing it, but if you look for clues connected to being underground and put yourself in the right kind of situation you'll be giving destiny a helping hand to connect you with the man you're meant to be with.

2. Get Spooky

As a Water sign you're exceptionally intuitive. Your gut instincts are often spot on and you sometimes seem to have an almost telepathic link with the people who are closest to you.

With such a strong, almost psychic sense you're very likely to have an affinity with things that go bump in the night.

It's possible that Halloween, scary movies, ghost stories and haunted houses hold a strange fascination for you. Whether such things appall you or enthrall you, and chances are it's a little of both, getting in touch with your spooky side is a great way for your sign to connect with your Significant Other.

It could be as simple as choosing to go and see a chiller rather than a romantic comedy if you're planning a trip to the movies. It's obvious that you'll have more chance of meeting an eligible guy lining up to see a movie that guys would willingly watch, rather than sitting through a chick flick marathon.

And if you're planning a movie night at home with friends make sure you invite guys as well as girls and rent *The Sixth Sense* or *The Village* or something more recent that appeals to your kind of spooky taste on DVD. There's no need to give yourself nightmares as it's not about watching gore, unless that kind of fear factor floats your boat. It's more about otherworldly experiences that make you jump out of your skin but laugh at yourself straight afterwards for doing so.

We've already established that a little bit of fear heightens the emotions and helps bonding, so this could be a way to make it work for you in the comfort of your own home.

At the theater, opt for seeing productions like the eerie *The Woman in Black* or *The Addams Family Musical* where you could meet guys who are on your wavelength too.

Another option is to book yourself onto a ghost walking tour or a ghost hunting night at a reputedly haunted house. The chance to look around someone else's dwelling appeals to the home-maker part of your personality but this adds a whole new element to the experience. Whether you encounter anything out of the ordinary or not, you could find yourself drawn to the handsome ghost hunter, or to the cute guy who happens to be there as a spectator too. Sharing your experiences afterwards could result in an uncannily romantic connection between you both.

And if you're going solo to a Halloween party think about turning up in costume as the other half of a famous spooky duo. You could find the Gomez to your Morticia Addams, or the Fred to your Daphne from *Scooby Doo*. Remember that even Frankenstein had a bride! You don't have to scare yourself to death in the process but you may be able to successfully scare yourself up a romantic partner.

3. Get Investigating

If you're true to your sign, one of the things that may keep you entertained is solving mysteries. It's partly to do with your legendary intuition which helps you sense when something's not quite right. But this is not about personal intrigues, it's more to do with the sheer pleasure of working out 'whodunnit' in a movie, TV show or murder mystery novel.

If you have a thing about crime novels you're not alone and it would make perfect sense to go on a crime fiction seminar to meet your favorite authors and fellow fiction fans, with the possibility of tracking down one who might turn out to be the romantic hero of your own life story.

You might even be inspired to be a modern day Agatha

Christie and write a crime novel of your own, something that could be life changing and beneficial in so many ways. If this sounds odd to you, bear in mind that your astrological zone being activated for love also rules creativity and taking a chance, and part of the idea of trying out new things is to take you out of your usual routine and to see yourself and others in a new light. When you're buzzing with excitement about doing something new it translates into a very attractive energy that others, potential love interests especially, pick up on. So even if you don't get into print, someone you meet on a crime writing course could turn out to be your Mr. Right.

If TV's crime solving show *CSI* fascinates you with its mix of forensics and foul play then you could think about investigating CSI: The Experience in Las Vegas on a vacation trip. In London, you might detect a love interest at a visit to 221b Baker Street, home of fictional detective Sherlock Holmes. And the Justice and Police Museum in Sydney is again an unusual but potentially fertile hunting ground for love. The theme that connects all of these is solving mysteries, so put your own spin on it and find that connection closer to home, and you'll still be on the right lines.

One way to do this is to invite friends, and single friends of friends, over for a murder mystery night where you get to dress up, play different characters and work out 'whodunnit'. Ready-made party packs are available to help you do this, and it's your chance to reveal your hidden depths. Since it's your party, choose to play the role of a sexy femme fatale as you want your sultry side to be on show.

And if you get the chance to attend a social function connected to law enforcement, get dressed up and go. You could find yourself handcuffed for life, in the nicest way possible, to a handsome detective.

4. Get Wet

As a Water sign, you're at your best in or near your natural element. You'll feel empowered when you're by a river, in or on the sea or even sitting by a water feature in your own garden.

To make the most of that, and to increase your chances of finding love, try to arrange to be in a watery situation on your best love days.

You have multiple options here. You could be on vacation by the beach, or on a cruise. The best times for romance for you are after dark as the kind of man who's likely to be your soulmate prefers moody, sensual surroundings rather than loud, raucous settings. So a candle-lit beach bar could be just the place to meet him.

There's a special connection for you in being beneath water in some way, which could mean you find him when you're visiting an aquarium, which is perfect for the symbol of your sign, the crab. With sharks and brightly colored tropical fish swimming around and above you behind glass, this could be the setting for a surprisingly low lit and lovely romantic encounter.

An equally unusual but equally worthwhile alternative is to visit a submarine museum. There are 25 of these in the USA alone and they provide the perfect scenario of being below water, plus a submarine is potentially more of a guys' interest so you're more likely to almost literally bump into someone who could be your future love, in this compact undersea world.

You could take a more conventional route to romance by going on a river boat cruise, but add a twist by doing it at Halloween and you're doubling your chances as this ties in with your 'Get Spooky' option too. University towns in the UK often offer guided tours on punts down the local river on the last night of October, and even if that doesn't coincide with your best love dates your chances of finding romance are still enhanced as your potential love match resonates well with this time of year.

If you're traveling, Paris is seen as a city of romance but your best bet for finding love there would be to take a tour of its infamous sewers. That hardly sounds romantic, but remember this is all about being in the right location to enhance what can only be described as your astrological love vibration. And it's more likely to happen for you on a sewer tour than, for example, at the Eiffel Tower. It's also possible to explore subterranean Seattle or the sewers in Sydney in Australia, and in the UK you could check out similar historical gems in quirky coastal Brighton. So you don't need to spend a fortune on going abroad to link with these places, just look for similar opportunities closer to home.

And if sewers don't do it for you, then if you're a sporty type scuba diving or snorkeling fit the bill for finding love too.

5. Get Practical

While it would be fantastic to have a great story to tell about how you met the man of your dreams, it's true to say that more often these life-changing encounters occur in the most mundane places.

For instance, in your case, there's high potential for finding love at your recycling center.

Because your intuitive and nurturing sign tends to care about the planet and you want to leave the world in good shape for future generations to enjoy, you're often drawn to other people who feel the same way. So why wouldn't you be eyeing up the guy who's crushing cans, squashing plastic bottles and folding his cardboard packets to help save planet Earth? He could be an eco friendly hunk who you click with as you're recycling wine bottles, or the man who runs the whole recycling operation in your town who you meet by chance over a glass of wine (but tie it in with your best love days and it will be more by design than by chance).

Your sign also tends to be good at making things, and anywhere you can recycle or upcycle homewares or jewelry from other people's junk is also the kind of place you may find a perfect partner. It could be at a craft or design fair, where he could be selling jewelry he's made from sea glass, shards from broken bottles that have been worn down by the sea and sand into beautiful, gem-like stones. And that watery link would be another sign that he could be the one for you.

Or you might find him at a reclamation center where items rescued from abandoned houses or demolished buildings get spruced up, refurbished, rehomed and loved all over again. He could be doing up his own home and be looking for salvaged vintage door handles or he might work for a demolition crew bringing in reclaimed timber, you just need to tune in to possible links that let you know you're on the right romantic track.

The same can be said for other dull but necessary areas of life which may hold surprisingly vast potential for romance. So if your cleaning machines or household gadgets, especially washing machines or dishwashers, break down don't despair and don't dismiss the allure of the plumber who comes to fix them. He could turn out to be your partner for life.

You could meet him at the laundromat, or he could be the salesman helping you to choose a new deep-cleaning carpet steamer. Because you tend to be rather house proud, someone connected to renovating the cellar or putting in a damp-proofing course also has possibilities.

And if your drains get blocked do give the guy who turns up to clear them a second look. He may not be what you had in mind as a soulmate but anyone who comes to help your treasured home function efficiently should be worthy of instant hero status, and maybe so much more.

6. Get Healing

Your sign has an in-built gift for healing. Cancerians naturally give a huge amount of love and care, often without even being aware of it, so it may pay you to develop that further by learning an alternative or even mainstream healing therapy.

Reiki, deep Swedish massage, aromatherapy massage and acupuncture are especially good areas for you to study, as well as to experience for yourself. Not only will you meet new people as you learn, but you'll need volunteers to expand your experience and clientele too, so your pool of potential love matches gets bigger and better.

You might also be drawn to spiritual healing which can be developed in groups, which again raises your chances of meeting someone on your emotional wavelength. More men are finding they have a talent for this as they get in touch with their sensitive side, so you'll be connecting with guys who have similar interests as well as the potential to be your perfect partner.

In the more orthodox medical world you could consider training as a nurse or doctor (or you may already be on this path) and find love while you're learning or through your work. You may find you're particularly attracted by, as well as being attractive to, men who wield knives for a living.

This could be a surgeon, particularly one who works with children or specializes in obstetrics, or a doctor who works in gynecology (he doesn't have to be your gynecologist, although he might be).

If he's into alternative therapy then the one for you is more likely to be an acupuncturist, but he might also be the carpenter helping to renovate a hospital wing, the chef in a hospital canteen, or you might meet him at the pharmacy while you're getting a prescription filled.

He might even be your neighbor who's cut himself shaving and knocks on your door to ask for sticking plaster.

Don't rule out anyone who has even the slightest link with healing or with sharp implements, especially if the two are connected in a healthy way, and remember this is all about trying different things and meeting people who may be vastly outside your usual dating pool but who could be just right for you.

That said, we all need to visit the dentist at some time, so that's nothing new but you may be surprised to learn that you may feel an extraordinarily strong attraction to your dentist. It's not the easiest situation in which to strike up a conversation but it can happen. If you're a single parent and have children, taking them to a dental appointment could result in romance for you. But again the important thing here is the location, so you might just encounter your dream date with a perfect smile while you're waiting for your turn to be seen, in your dentist's waiting room.

7. Get Mystical

A fascination for some of the more alternative things in life goes hand in hand with being a Cancerian. Because you work on instinct, you're often more tuned into the natural world than others, even though you may be quite secretive about it for fear of being thought a little crazy. But you're currently reading a book on astrology so your secret's out!

And it's no coincidence that studying astrology, tarot or palmistry yourself could help you meet the right kind of guy.

Someone you can merge with emotionally and share your interests with is likely to be the sort of man you feel most at home with, a more sensitive soulmate rather than a macho-minded male who might dismiss some of your beliefs as nonsense. Because he's sensitive doesn't mean he's a delicate, shy and retiring type. It does mean he's a deep thinker who's going to be deeply attuned to your moods and your needs. He practically knows what you're thinking and may be particularly sensitive and attentive to what you like in bed too.

You might find him teaching, or studying with you on a course. You might contact him for a reading, or he could contact you for the same thing once you're proficient, and you'll just know that he's 'the one'. There's a strong sense of karmic connection for you with the man you're destined to hook up with.

You might decide to expand your already fabulous intuition

on a psychic development course, where you might find him, or once you've learned to tune in you could develop an instinct about the kinds of places and situations you're most likely to get lucky in love as you're quite likely to sense him before you actually see him.

You might meet your match at a Mind, Body and Spirit fair. It's not even essential that he's connected to all things mystical, he could be there helping to put up exhibition stands, or to support a friend who's exhibiting. The main link is the location, though there is a good chance that the man for you does have more than a passing interest in alternative therapies, fascinating ideas on nutrition (which is another area that will help you gel) and an unusual lifestyle.

Because food and nurturing are important to you, you could encounter him at a farmers market. He'll be the one with the stall selling organic fruit and vegetables, possibly even grown and harvested by the phases of the moon. Your sign is ruled by the moon so someone who understands how the moon affects plants is more likely to get why you're so ruled by your emotions at times, which makes him definite partner material.

Others often see you as an incredibly practical person, so you may have had a tendency to deny your affinity with things and ideas that may seem 'off the wall' to them. Common sense has little to do with finding love, but relying on your sixth sense and trusting your instincts can help you tune into and find your soulmate, especially when the planets are aligning to help romance along.

Location Checklist

A checklist is a handy way to get focused and pinpoint those places you need to add to your routine in order to help love along. This is not an exhaustive list by any means but will give you some ideas, and help you think of many more along similar lines. You could meet 'the one' at a:

- Crime novel writing course
- Scary film
- Mining exhibition
- Haunted house
- Recycling center
- Murder mystery night
- Underground nightclub
- Mind, Body & Spirit fair
- Astrology course
- Acupuncture course
- Pharmacy
- Hospital
- DIY store, plumbing section
- Halloween party
- Reclamation center
- Dentist's surgery
- Subway train
- Potholing

When you've found your perfect partner, look back on this and smile at the memory of the time you were on the subway and got talking to a cute guy about recycling. He worked at a reclamation center and offered to find you that claw-foot tub you've always wanted. He plumbed it in for you, and you christened it together decadently with champagne and aromatherapy bath oils! And the rest is history. Insert your own romantic 'how we met' story instead, of course.

Chapter 5

Where to Find Love if You're Leo

Leos love to be adored, worshipped even, as befits their status as astrological royalty. Your sign is ruled by the Sun, the head honcho in the planetary line-up, and where would all the other planets and signs be without the Sun or you at the center of their universe?

Well, here's the thing. In life, as in astrology and in relationships especially, it's not all about you.

Hard as it may be to see that in print, since you adore being the main attraction, this self-centeredness you sometimes display can mean that your potential Significant Other doesn't get a look in when it comes to romance.

You're incredible fun to be around but your strong presence can be overpowering at times, especially if you feel you're not being heard, are being overlooked or are simply not getting your own way.

Making a relationship work needs a certain amount of equality and compromise, neither of which comes easily to your sign.

Lovers in the past may have tended to tread on eggshells around you, not wanting to upset you or hear you roar with displeasure for any minor misdemeanor on their part, but this has perhaps contributed to your ongoing belief that it's your way or the highway.

Or your usual kind of partner may have become so immune to your attention-seeking ways that he's eventually distanced himself from you emotionally or physically, which may have made you even more of a drama queen to get the attention you crave.

Part of the problem is you often hide behind your public face, so others rarely get to see the real you. You tend to use drama and theatrical gestures as a mask to protect your child-like and vulnerable side from being seen and getting hurt.

So, your mission is to step away from the guys who may be cute, cutting edge and cool but who may also be too aloof, independent and unpredictable to really last the distance with you anyway. Instead, look for a man who has your same large appetite for life and laughter, and who will take any of your occasional drama queen antics in his stride.

Tears and tantrums won't work with him so you won't be able to twist him around your little finger. And he's honest to the point of bluntness so it could come as a shock to find this warm, wonderful, witty and wise man can play you at your own game, and win by playing fair.

As a result you'll open up to him like you've never opened up to anyone before, so there's no need for pretense or keeping up appearances. You can just be authentically you.

And as your sign loves to be entertained as well as to be entertaining, from now on your quest for a soulmate becomes more enjoyable than it probably has been for some time.

Each of the following options is a way to put you in the path of destiny and help you find your perfect partner. You may not even need to try all of them if things go right first time, but give them a go anyway for the sheer hell and pleasure of it. You'll come out of the experience a more well-rounded person or, as you might see it, become even more fabulous than you already are.

In astrology, Leo rules the heart, so when you feel that internal click of connection with someone special, you'll know that you're in the right place at the right time to make things last.

1. Get Away

One of the best places for you to find love is on vacation, or at least somewhere that's far from your usual territory. That may sound like a challenge but with cheap flights and the internet, you have nothing to lose by looking further afield for your dream man.

As you're currently reading an astrological guide to love you're clearly open to using astrology to find your soulmate, so to pinpoint where to go to find him you could ask your friendly astrologer at www.orlilysen.com for a relocation chart. This will show you where on the planet you're most likely to have a life-changing romantic experience.

It's all about picking up on the energy of whichever country resonates best for you astrologically. If you can spend time in the country that elevates your love luck that's the best option but if time, money and distance really are a problem, you may not even have to travel there to start the romantic ball rolling.

For instance, if your relocation chart connects you romantically to Paris you could start going to French restaurants near where you live, go on a course to learn French, or hook up with a Parisian guy on an internet dating site and invite him over to visit you or the other way around. In fact all you need to do is tune into what can only be described as a Parisian love vibration. He might be French but in the same country as you. He doesn't even have to be French but he might be into French things so you could encounter him at a cinema where a French subtitled movie is playing. This may sound odd but it actually works. You just need to know which country (or countries) work their magic for you.

Otherwise just keep it simple and head somewhere sunny that you like the sound of and, so long as the stars are in the right place at the right time for you to find love, let destiny take its course.

Getting away to learn something new is also a good idea for you as rather than just chilling out by the pool it's by meeting up with others with a shared interest that you may be put on a direct route to making a deeper, lasting connection. This could be by doing a yoga instructor's course, learning to teach a foreign language abroad or working at an international summer camp for kids.

Men linked to travel could also float your boat. You could connect romantically with the captain of the ship if you're on a cruise, or an airline pilot or steward. It could be the travel agent who helped you book your trip, or the travel rep who's devastatingly handsome as well as devastatingly knowledgeable about the country you're visiting. It could even be the guy who sold you your suitcase.

All you need to do is look for connections to travel, and romance won't be far behind.

2. Get Laughing

Your sign has a terrific sense of humor and Leos love to laugh, so in the quest for love think about going to a comedy night at a venue near you or, better still, to an international comedy festival.

The buzz of a live performance raises your endorphins, the body's natural mood enhancers, much more than just by watching comedy home alone on TV, and shared laughter adds to the feelgood factor too.

Comedy venues are fabulous places for your sign to make a love connection. There's a good 'guy to gal' mix, usually with more men than women, so your chances of hooking up are automatically increased.

As you tend to love being on show and stealing the limelight you may find you become part of the routine if you're brave enough to heckle, or if you sit close enough to the stage to get singled out for attention by the performers.

If you really get a feel for this you might even think you can do better, so why not have a go at comedy yourself? This would be really pushing anyone's boundaries but you of all people could cope with it, since you're a natural performer.

Being in the spotlight is clearly a fantastic way to get noticed and be adored, but in order to have people laugh with you and not at you, you need to learn how to be funny. Studying something you love that's also fun is more important than you may realize for your sign, as learning anything that expands your knowledge and your horizons is more likely to put you in touch with the love of your life.

And even if you never make it onto the stage, your shared learning curve with other would-be stand-ups could be a highly bonding, potentially romantic thing. You could even end up writing a comedy novel, or be on TV or in a magazine being interviewed about your hilarious attempts to learn a stand-up routine, which could also get you noticed by potential admirers.

More down to earth but probably more likely is the possibility that you'll just feel more confident that, if asked, you can give a memorable and funny speech at a friend's wedding, where there will undoubtedly be single, available guys.

This whole comedy experience is partly about making yourself more visible but also about allowing your vulnerability to show, and being able to laugh at yourself too. Because for Leos, and the ideal man for you, laughter is the ultimate aphrodisiac.

3. Get Spiritual

Connecting to something soulful is a great way to open up your world and let someone new into it. It also involves being mindful of others as much, if not more, than you are of your own needs.

Forward-thinking, fund-raising faith-based organizations are realizing that the way to attract more people is to make things more fun. So social events, quiz nights, comedy nights, film shows or dances held in religious buildings could be where your skills and interests may be put to good use, and where you could find romance.

These events might be connected to a religious group but also look out for things happening in converted or deconsecrated churches: Mind-expanding art exhibitions, live music or retro DJ nights and more. Remember, in astrology it's the location that's a vital link for meeting your potential soulmate too.

Well-known musicians occasionally play gigs in cathedrals as the acoustics are amazing so, again, look for unusual entertainments that appeal to you that are taking place in ecclesiastical surroundings. You might encounter someone special who could open up your world romantically and restore your faith in love.

If that doesn't tempt you, you might feel more drawn to alternative forms of spirituality. You don't have to become affiliated to a particular belief system to enjoy and be part of what's going on. So you might love gospel singing but you needn't be a member of the church, or you might want to try meditation but you don't have to become a Buddhist.

Meditation, in fact, would be ideal for you, to help quieten your chattering mind and focus on attaining what you really want from life and love.

Look for more spiritual types of exercise too, like tai chi or chi gung, where you could also encounter a more thoughtful kind of guy. You may find you connect romantically with your tutor or with a guru-like figure who helps you to lighten up as you learn, and brings a simpler state of happiness into your world.

Or you could join a yoga class where esoteric knowledge, if you choose to take it on board, combines with health and fitness. Be aware that guys are more likely to go for the more strenuous types of yoga such as Ashtanga or Bikram. It's faster, hotter and harder but makes you leaner and trimmer in double quick time, so it's worth investigating if you want to combine fitness and spirituality with the potential to meet a soulmate.

The right man for you might be spiritual but he's also up for some fun. So to meet him you could try aerial yoga, where you get to perform yoga moves while suspended in a silk hammock. This would appeal to the performer in you as you'll get to do flips and tricks too and it has the added benefit of attracting fit guys, as cyclists and mountain climbers in particular seem drawn to this yoga style.

4. Get Noticed

If you're true to your sign you rather like a little publicity and self-promotion. This should come fairly easily to you as you're not usually shy, but in order to meet the man who's right for you, you need to get yourself noticed on a bigger and bolder scale.

If you're involved with a drama group (and if you're not then give it a try) aim for the leading role or a part that gets attention, ideally a comedy role as the man for you loves to laugh. And if you are shy with guys, a one-on-one session with a drama coach could help you combat your fears and give you the confidence you need to make a connection with someone special.

Broadcasting the fact that you're looking for love is nothing to be shy about so if you're trying internet dating, which is a particularly good way for you to meet your match, make your profile stand out. Bigger, better, brighter and funnier are your key words here. Think about having a professional photo taken and wear something bright, though keep your look natural as the ideal man for you hates pretense and anything artificial.

If you'd rather not be on show, make your words-only personal dating ad witty. This is the way to help find you a word-loving lover, and if you can make him smile you're half way to his heart already.

If you feel particularly bold, you could have a better chance than most of hooking up with someone through a matchmaking feature in a magazine or on a TV dating show.

Getting tickets for your favorite TV talk show or comedy show is not so hard, and if there's any kind of audience participation you could get noticed by someone who likes the way you come across on-screen, or you could find yourself sitting next to the man of your dreams in the audience.

Still in the public eye, you could meet him at a marketing

networking event or be approached by the cute guy in the street with the clipboard, doing a survey to taste-test a new brand of orange juice.

You could apply to be an extra in a movie, another great place to meet someone who has similar tastes and dreams to you. He could be an actor, director or potentially even the horse wrangler if it's a western or historical drama.

And if there's something you're connected with that you'd like to promote, your local radio station could be the place to get your message heard and help you find love in the process. Broadcasters and DJs suit your sign extraordinarily well.

So think about media, advertising and promotion when you're looking for the love of your life. You're the best commodity you have so it's a great way to let the world know what a fabulous 'one-time only' offer you are.

5. Get Adventurous

Channel your inner Lara Croft or Indiana Jones and go on an adventure. This is more than just a vacation, think of it as a quest. Be bold, be brave, be daring and take some time out to do something worthwhile that perhaps helps others while you're at it.

It could be a sponsored charity trek up a mountain or an endurance race across the desert. Even an organized adventure trip to somewhere that thrills and scares you in equal measures fits the bill. Or you could volunteer to teach the work or life skills you have overseas.

You might be more used to living a luxurious lifestyle, but camping, trekking or roughing it for a while is character-building stuff, and again helps you to let go of the need for whatever emotional security blankets you hide the real you behind to get you through each day.

A safari or, better still, the chance to work with animals on a game reserve, is a fabulous choice for you as it brings out your animal magnetism too. But even an adventure closer to home where you get to experience a more rugged, outdoorsy style of living could work wonders for you and your love life.

Survival, being personally challenged, broadening your outlook and being a team player are what this experience is all about. You could meet a handsome conservationist, an inspirational tour guide or even fall for the guy in charge of the lions at a game park, though probably not a lion tamer as it's unlikely that anyone is ever likely to truly tame you, Ms. Leo.

You could try combining adventure travel with a more soulful element that ties into your 'Get Spiritual' options too for a double whammy, perhaps heading off to India to study yoga, or making a pilgrimage to a sacred place like Machu Picchu in Peru. If you do you'll be more likely to meet the kind of guy who, while spiritual, is part fiery action man too rather than a wistful dreamer.

You could blog or put together an enlightening 'how you did it' e-book about your experiences, as sharing information and knowledge plays a big part for you in connecting with the right guy.

If this sounds like it's way out of your comfort zone then pare it down to what's doable and practical. Can't go on safari? See if you can volunteer to help out at your local zoo.

Finding your ideal partner is about evolving to become the kind of interesting person you'd like to attract into your life. As a Leo you have very high standards so it's reasonable to assume that the kind of man you want has high standards too, so the more you can do to be 'partner ready' when you meet him, the better.

6. Get Sporty

Sport, whether you're watching it or playing it, offers you a great opportunity to win a romantic partner.

Horse riding, show jumping and polo in particular are the

targets to aim for. You love to dress up and look the part whatever you do, so putting on a Barbour jacket and jodhpurs, even if you've no intention of riding, may fulfill some of your fantasies about living the high life.

Hanging out with the horsey set could put you in touch with a man who owns or breeds thoroughbreds, but you could just as easily fall for a groom who could one day end up as your groom as he walks you down the aisle.

The world of horse racing is also worth a gamble as anything with added chance and a calculated risk heightens the odds of you finding the perfect partner. Watching racing on TV could even bring love your way if you're with the right crowd.

If that's not your thing, then a pony trek somewhere hilly and scenic could work just as well, and this also puts you in touch with your adventurous side. Helping out at riding stables or a horse or donkey sanctuary is another way to help you connect with your future love.

Equally effective would be to try your hand at archery. Part of this whole experience is about attempting things you might never have thought of doing before, and this could be a real test of your pulling power in every way. You do have quite a competitive streak, so your aim would be to hit the bulls-eye as well as to pierce a fellow archer's heart, but only with Cupid's arrows.

This could also work for you at a costume party. Someone dressed as Robin Hood, William Tell, the superhero The Green Arrow or even Cupid himself may well be the man you're looking for. So follow the arrows as, symbolically, wherever you see them is a potential sign that you're heading in the right direction for love.

Taking a risk or a gamble has already been mentioned and, for Leos, there's a real element of luck involved with finding your Mr. Right, so let synchronicity (coincidences) and serendipity (happy accidents) be your watchwords. So long as you get your timing right and are looking for romance on your best love days, especially when Jupiter's working in your favor, there are good odds for the stars putting you exactly where you're meant to be to meet the person you're meant to be with forever.

7. Get Wise

Your sign is often more attracted by looks, outward appearance and by Alpha males, but attraction can be as much about stimulating the mind as it can be about the body.

There's a special link between love and education for you so consider stretching yourself to learn something amazing that fascinates you, especially if you can share it with others.

Particularly good areas to consider trying are Open University courses in law or philosophy. Either of these would put you among the kind of man that would suit you beautifully.

And as cutting across cultural barriers is a key element for finding your soulmate too he may be from a different country so think about learning a new language, and listen out for his sexy accent.

Whatever you study doesn't have to be intellectual but it should be fun and enjoyable, and again, made for sharing. Learning to cook international cuisine could be more your thing, from rustling up the perfect Italian meal to something more exotic like a Moroccan tagine, Mexican feast or Indian buffet. Classes in any of these could help you meet 'the one'. And going on a vacation where you learn to cook doubles your chances of finding love as you'll be combining travel with gaining knowledge, two things the ideal man for you adores.

You might instead take a course in tour guiding. Whether it's showing people around the arts and entertainments scene, historical sites or fabulous countryside in your local area or somewhere hot and far away, either would put you in the right place for romance.

And as communication in all its forms is a key element of your search for Mr. Right you could try a course in storytelling, for children or adults. It's an ideal outlet for you as you'd get to entertain (since you'll officially be the center of attention) and you'll open up your dating world to guys who'll love to listen to you, as well as talk with and entertain you.

Anything connected to the media would be a great way for you to meet your soulmate too. Attending a presentation skills workshop for your job, or learning about PR or advertising to advance your own sideline business into becoming your main source of income offers strong potential for you to meet your Significant Other. Demonstrating your creative skills, if you're a potter or an artist, or even working as an in-store demonstrator could also help you catch someone's romantic eye.

You could even train to be a teacher yourself and run education classes for adults in your favorite subject.

All you have to do to find love is connect love and learning. So don't dismiss that geeky tutor who has a heart of gold, or even the guy you were at college with who seemed like a nerd back then, but is now all grown up and a genius.

And it doesn't mean you actually have to study. If you're day-tripping to a university town or just taking your kids (if you have them) to school on your best love days, love could turn out to be on your curriculum.

Location Checklist

A checklist is a handy way to focus your direction and pinpoint those places you need to add to your routine in order to help love along. This is not an exhaustive list but will give you the idea, and help you think of many more along similar lines. You could meet 'the one' at a:

- Yoga class
- Vacation
- Adventure trip
- Media networking event

- TV show
- Internet
- Archery lesson
- Showjumping event
- Horse racing
- Costume party
- Polo match
- Machu Picchu
- Safari
- Comedy club
- Stand-up comedy course
- Church fund-raiser
- Concert at a cathedral
- Film location

When you've found your perfect partner, look back on this and smile at the memory of the time you took archery lessons. As you felt the tutor's arms around you when he showed you how to pull back the bow you knew he was something special, but it was the way he made you laugh at a comedy open mic night that clinched the deal. After an adventure trek across the desert to see the Pyramids in Egypt you became inseparable. And the rest is history. Insert your own romantic 'how we met' story instead, of course.

Chapter 6

Where to Find Love if You're Virgo

Yours is the most practical sign of the zodiac. As a Virgo you're the go-to girl for any kind of information as your sources are accurate and your facts are spot on (you'll have checked them at least twice).

You're often a walking encyclopedia when it comes to health and are a great person to have around in a crisis as your efficient manner gets the job done without turning the situation into a drama.

If only your love-life could be managed in such a no-nonsense way. The trouble is because you're so cool, calm and collected you often attract men who are completely the opposite. Dreamy, unfocused, poetic and undoubtedly romantic, these lost souls seem to attach themselves to you to anchor them in their sea of fantasy.

Your inner strength is irresistible to guys with addictive personalities, and you may find that men who seem like hopeless cases or who lean on alcohol or drugs to get through life are magnetically drawn to you. These are extreme examples but you can probably make a list of ex-boyfriends who were particularly needy in some way.

The thing is, you like a project and if anyone can improve or mend a situation, person or thing you have a firm belief that that person is you.

Not any more. In your quest for the man of your dreams, the men who are lost in their own delusions have to go. Instead, you're going to be looking for someone who's strong-minded, respected, stable and going up in the world, if he hasn't made it to the top of his field already. This kind of guy may have been on your wish list for some while but you've been too busy helping out the waifs and strays to find him.

He'll like your precise ways and your attention to detail, but don't think he won't challenge you to raise your game, which is something you may not be used to. He'll want to be proud of you, not as a trophy girlfriend or wife but as someone who's smart in every sense and accomplished in her career or as a homemaker or both.

In turn, you'll want to look after him, but not by being a doormat, which may have been the case in other relationships. Your sign loves to be of service, even if you're the boss at work, by giving help, advice, and offering practical and grounded solutions to life's problems. Rather than having these gifts abused or taken advantage of, your ideal man will value your opinion and give you credit for all you do.

So how will you recognize this wonderful guy when you encounter him? He might be creative, like your dreamy past loves, but he'll be successful, not struggling. He's likely to be the boss or owner of where he works. He could be maturely handsome in a craggy way, or youthful but with an old head on young shoulders. He's got his feet on the ground, but he's planning his next step up the ladder.

If your timing is right, and with your usual Virgoan efficiency by checking your best love times it will be, there's nothing stopping you finding your perfect partner so long as you look for him in all the right places.

1. Get Working

If you're a typical Virgo you love your work. It's often a pleasure for you to get up and start the morning so you can put in a good day at the office (or wherever) and come home satisfied.

It's great to find fulfillment in your job, after all you spend enough hours of the day doing it and then a few more thinking about it, so you might as well be doing something you enjoy. But life can't be all work and no play, can it?

So the easiest and possibly the best option for you when it comes to romance is to consider dating a colleague. Much as you'd rather not mix business with pleasure, because you are something of a workaholic it does make sense that your pool of possible dates includes those you work with.

Interestingly enough, you're more likely to be attracted either to senior management, who may have their eye on you anyway as you're a star performer at what you do, or a younger employee who you may be mentoring.

Obviously you'll want to be discreet and professional at all times, but don't rule this option out.

On the plus side you get to know what he's like on a day-to-day basis, both at his best and under pressure. The possible downside is if it all goes wrong or alternatively all goes wonderfully right, do you still work together or does one of you have to move on to job opportunities elsewhere? With your analytical mind you'll already be thinking of a Plan B for this just in case.

In a company environment it may be better to have some personal space so, if you can, find someone in a different department or even a local branch office rather than your own.

If it does all turn out to be fantastic you might want to take the element of working together a step further and perhaps set up your own business as a couple. Great areas for you to explore are alternative therapies, making things by hand, and research and property development or renovation, so they may be something you diversify into doing once you've got your man, or you might want to look into these now if you fancy a career change.

Employment agencies and career advisory services may also be where you connect with someone special if you're thinking about changing your job. And if you're happy where you are make sure you network at business events connected to what you do, as this is another avenue where you could find your future prospects are better, and more romantic, than you could have imagined.

2. Get Climbing

Hit the heights! The man of your dreams is a high flyer so where do you go to find him? Climbing hills and mountains is a good start.

If you've never done this before, you might like to set yourself a challenge such as climbing a mountain or doing a hill walk for charity.

If you do, you'll need to get into shape and one of the best ways to do this is with the kind of fitness training that takes you up hills and down dales. It's tough going, but you're very driven and your powers of endurance, once you've made up your mind to do something, are admirable. The unstinting, determined and authoritative kind of man who will help you get the fitness results you need could also turn out to be the man for you.

You could instead try a climbing wall at a local leisure center, or if you're a single parent, take your kids there as there are likely to be plenty of single dads doing the same thing, hopefully a few of them fit enough to climb the wall themselves.

There's a lot of trust involved in any sort of climbing as you're often tethered to a partner or a team so one decision affects all. That's also the way you like to operate in life, being aware of the needs of others, so it makes sense that this principle factors into your leisure time and romance too.

High places and places of power are also a draw for the kind of man who would suit you. In London check out The Shard, the tallest building in Western Europe, or if you're on vacation think about visiting the Eiffel Tower in Paris. The view from the Empire State Building (watch *Sleepless in Seattle* and *An Affair to Remember* on DVD for inspiration) may get you into a suitably romantic mood. Alternatively you could visit the Eureka Tower in Australia or explore the world's tallest building, the Burj Khalifa in Dubai.

If these are too far afield, think about the places nearer to you where you can get a bird's eye view of the surroundings. There's every possibility that the perfect man will be there admiring it with you.

You could even try social climbing, which is not really your thing as you tend to be very down to earth and too genuine to sweet talk your way into the social circles of the elite, but the man for you is quite possibly someone you may consider to be out of your usual league, so you'd do well to rub shoulders at the kind of events where he can be found.

Invest in tickets for a high profile charity event or a fundraising affair and go and mingle. You may even find that offering to help out behind the scenes could put you in the right place at the right time to catch Mr. Right's eye.

3. Get Building

If you're a home owner and are looking to make some changes, while you're about it look to the men who may be renovating your property as they could also be laying the groundwork for love.

There's a very strong likelihood that you could gel with a man connected to the building industry. He could be an architect or a bricklayer, or someone who's repairing the roof or chimney, possibly even someone who's come to sweep your chimney if you live in an older property.

You don't have to be the owner of the building, or even live there. It could be the place you live next door to or pass by every day on the way to work. Just be aware of wherever extensions, renovations and building work in general are being carried out in your vicinity because these are signs that love may be in the air.

As yours is an Earth sign you like the feel of anything that's solid and stable, and the same goes for men who are in the business of providing stability both literally, in the form of strong foundations for a building, or financially, for a home and family in the future.

You could even have a romantic encounter while viewing

plans for local building developments in your area, if you bump into someone there who could have plans on getting together with you.

You could meet him at a home design exhibition, or at a company that sells property. A romance with a real estate agent is a strong possibility, especially if he deals in buildings that are of special architectural interest, perhaps a brand new development or more likely a property that's an historically fascinating fixer-upper which would be exactly your kind of project.

Even a trip to your local DIY store could end with romance if you time your visit to coincide with your best love days.

4. Get Crafty

By crafty, it's not about being devious, although you're such a smart cookie if there's someone you like the look of you're clever enough to find a way to get him into your life sooner or later.

Rather you should pursue some creative avenues to make sure you encounter him.

Your sign has a real affinity with making things that are useful. Designer William Morris once said you should only own things you believe to be beautiful or know to be useful. This could be your mantra as generally you don't like fuss or frippery but are not averse to having something rather lovely with which to do a practical job.

So you might consider taking up pottery. Plant pots and containers are, to your sign, extremely useful as you're the kind of gal who's likely to have a collection of herbs for well-being that you want to grow and present in an attractive and orderly way.

You could hit it off with the pottery teacher, or if you don't feel the desire to make pots yourself it's quite possible you may fall for a potter while you're searching for practical, pretty and perfectly-priced plant containers.

Any kind of craft or design fair is a great place for you to visit or to show your own creations, for ideas and inspiration as well as to make some useful purchases or sales and even more useful romantic connections. You might find a whole host of guys who are on your wavelength, as hand-made items and the men who make them really appeal to your senses.

Men who sculpt or make jewelry with precious or semi-precious stones could also be particularly attractive to you, especially if there's an element of recycling involved as your sign is usually very eco conscious.

5. Get Historical

With your sign, your ruling planet Mercury brings out your analytical mind. You ponder things deeply, soak up information as naturally as breathing, and apply rational thought to devise practical solutions that are designed to last.

Although you're often very clued up about what's going on and what's current and popular, in your heart you're a bit of a traditionalist. And so is the man of your dreams, which is where your supreme organizational skills come in to play to help you find love.

He could be involved with preserving historical properties, working with ancient manuscripts in a museum or specialist library, or preserving traditional skills that might otherwise fade into oblivion.

Because you think and work so efficiently, you could get involved in any of these areas, which are always in need of funds, to rally other people around to help too. You'd be great at organizing staff rotas, clean up campaigns, fund-raising or just being a friendly, helpful presence to guide visitors around.

Volunteering your services in any capacity that you feel comfortable with and useful in can help make an impression on the right kind of man for you who may also be volunteering, though he's more likely to be heading up the project or to be involved as an interested spectator or investor.

When it comes to preserving the past, odd as it may sound, candle making is a very specific if unusual area that your future love may be involved with. Because you're such a hands-on person too, picking up practical skills like this could help you forge a romantic bond with someone special.

There's no point getting involved with something that doesn't make your heart sing, and finding the love of your life should be a fun and rewarding experience, so adapt these ideas to suit you and your lifestyle.

For instance, a walking tour of a city, whether it's in your own country or abroad (fabulous Venice is crumbling away so could be just the place) is another way to get acquainted with someone who's on your wavelength. He could be the tour guide, someone else on the tour or a cute guy that you encounter as you stroll around hidden places in your own town that you may never have been to before.

Strange as it may sound, Mr. Right might also have a fascination for cemeteries, and headstones in particular. He could be tracing his family tree or just be intrigued by the weird, wonderful and often beautiful ways that people choose to be remembered. Or he could be the guy responsible for tending the cemetery land and keeping things in order.

It's not as spooky as you might think. If you're traveling through Paris take a detour to Père Lachaise, the final resting place of assorted celebrities. Buenos Aires in Argentina has a stunning cemetery in La Recoleta, and New Orleans and Mexico have fascinating shrines that are worth a visit. Remember that the location is important, as it's about putting you in the right place at the right time to meet the right guy.

So the key elements for finding your man are places with a sense of history, authority and longevity, which kind of sums him up as well. He likes things that are built to last and he wants to build a dynasty so this guy, once you've found him, is a keeper.

6. Get Down On The Farm

Getting in touch with your earthy side can work wonders for your love life.

As a rule, you're into all things clean and hygienic but if it means getting down and dirty in the pursuit of work or love, then you're the type to just roll up your sleeves and get on with it.

Virgo has a strong affinity with small farm or domestic animals as, potentially, does the man who could rock your world. He might be a gentleman farmer with a business that's been in the family for generations and he'd like to keep it that way, or someone who owns or runs a petting zoo for children. A rare breeds center, with small farm animals or more exotic creatures, is also a possibility as this guy is passionate about saving animals which might otherwise become endangered or even extinct.

To narrow your search, look for goats, in particular as a sign that you're on the right track with this man. Again, it may sound odd but trust the astrology! To be in with a chance with you, he'll most likely run his farm as a place for making artisan goat's cheese, or run his zoo as an educational resource as well as a fun experience for school parties.

With your practical nature, you'd be an asset to either venture, as these kinds of businesses often need helpers to help run things which again suits your sign's willingness to be of service. And you may look like you're only helping out but the chances are you'll end up unofficially running the place.

Once you've shown how indispensable you are you could hook up with the owner, or a client or a teacher visiting the site.

If this all sounds like it's too much out of your comfort zone, look for simpler connections. You could both be reaching for the goat's cheese at the same time at the supermarket, or he could be selling goatskin rugs at a street market. You might find him at a pub or bar called 'The Goat and Compasses'. The links are there for you to put yourself in the right place for love, if you look for them.

7. Get Healthy

Doing what you love is one of the best ways to meet someone special. When you're focused on doing something you're passionate about, you don't have time to fixate on your lack of a boyfriend or life partner because you're so 'in the moment'.

Your sign is often very passionate about health. Whether you're currently in your best shape ever or are trying hard to get there, you're building up a vast knowledge of what does and doesn't work for you, and others, health-wise.

So learning a skill that benefits other people's health would put you completely in your comfort zone as well as in your romantic zone. It's quite possible that you may already be involved in this area, either simply for personal interest or as a professional healer in some way.

If you want to be in the right kind of place to meet the right kind of man, think about focusing on treatments that work on improving posture and anything to do with the skeleton, including studying to become a chiropractor.

That may sound like a big task especially if you're starting from scratch, but Virgos love a challenge, and have incredible endurance and capacity to absorb information.

Remember, too, to check your ideal love dates as they could be next week or they could be even better in a year or so, which gives you an incentive and a deadline to work to.

A quicker fix would be a therapeutic massage course, as the type of man who would be good for you may have a tendency towards sports injuries or occasional work-related aches and pains.

You're a natural healer so you could meet someone on a course, or while you're in the waiting room before having a treatment yourself. Romantic opportunities could also arise while you're visiting the dentist.

Finally, bizarre but true, another way to tune into your possible soulmate is via archeology. Although not strictly related to health, the study of archeology does link with the development of the human race.

The man of your dreams could be an archeologist, he could be teaching the subject or just be fascinated with human or even dinosaur bones. This also touches on the study of early tools, crafts, stone implements and pots so has multiple connections for practically-minded you and your partner-to-be. Where to find him? Hanging out at your nearest natural history museum or on an archeological dig offers the potential for hooking up with this fascinating guy.

Location Checklist

A checklist is a handy way to focus your direction and pinpoint those places you need to add to your routine in order to help love along. This is not an exhaustive list but will give you the idea, and help you think of many more along similar lines. You could meet 'the one' at a:

- Pottery class
- Sculpture exhibition
- Business networking seminar
- Hill walking
- Climbing wall
- Historic house
- Architect's office
- DIY store
- Social event at work
- Chiropractor's clinic
- Ancient monument
- Cemetery
- Farm
- Petting zoo
- Candle store
- Natural history museum

- Clean-up campaign
- Supermarket cheese counter

When you've found your perfect partner, look back on this and smile at the memory of the time you met that guy at the sculpture exhibition. He turned out to be the owner of a rare breeds zoo that needed help with fund-raising. Your amazing organizational skills saved the day and the animals, and before too long you got hitched to him at a fabulous historic house. And the rest is history. Insert your own romantic 'how we met' story instead, of course.

Chapter 7

Where to Find Love if You're Libra

As the most balanced sign of the zodiac, and the one most connected to relationships, it's ironic that the only thing that's likely to throw a Libran off kilter at times is romance.

While it's true you love to be surrounded by all that's simple, tasteful and elegant thanks to your ruling planet Venus, deep down you have a decidedly quirky side when it comes to love. Not that you're likely to admit it, even to yourself, and that could be where things have been a little shaky in the past.

Because as it turns out, people who stimulate your mind are just as likely, if not more, to make you adore them than those who appeal to your eyes.

But so strong is the pressure to have some eye candy on your arm, for your own visual pleasure as much as to impress anyone else who might be looking, that you may have overlooked other qualities that are the key to compatibility with you: Emotional depth and an unusual take on life that is unceasingly fascinating.

That doesn't always come in a designer-clad package, so are you prepared to compromise and let someone more unusual into your life, no matter how oddball or eccentric-looking they may be?

The chances are that in the past you've dated (or hankered after) strong-minded, traditional guys who look good and are (or like to think they are) Alpha males. After the initial attraction and allure, things may have fizzled out as they may have overwhelmed you or tried to dominate you, when what you really want is equality.

And if it feels like you change your boyfriends as often as you change your fashion accessories, the suggestions that follow about where to find love may surprise you. But that's the point.

True style is about being an individual, choosing what or who suits you, your mood and your taste, rather than going along with what anyone else dictates as being perfect.

There's no such thing as perfection, and beauty, even in precious gems, lies in the flaws and differences, not the uniformity of something mass-produced or synthetic. The same goes for your ideal partner, as true love is about loving someone because of their flaws, not despite them.

No one's dictating that you should lower your standards, but you of all signs, with your ability to see both sides of a situation and aim for a fair conclusion, should be aware that honesty is all. So be honest with yourself about who you really connect with and love will follow.

The other issue for your sign is often one of over-dependence upon your partner. It's not that you're needy but because Libra is the sign of relationships and is symbolized by the scales, you often feel unbalanced without someone else in your life.

For real and long-term success in a relationship it's worthwhile trying to cultivate a mindset of non-attachment to people and to things. Your ideal guy will help you to appreciate the beauty of independence, individuality and freedom within a loving union. Here's how and where you're most likely to meet him.

1. Get Connected

How are you with gadgets? You'll either love them or loathe them, in which case this is still a win-win situation.

If you have a cell phone, laptop or whatever the latest gadget is, get to the tech store and treat yourself to an upgrade or to something new to go with it.

Just an app will do, the key is to get talking to the sales team as there's a strong chance that you, more than most signs, can connect with guys who know their way around electrical wizardry.

This can also help you bond with any males you know socially, or in the IT department at work where all the techno geeks hang out.

Do not fear the word geek! Behind that mask lies a heart of gold and a need to be loved just as much as you do. Think of these men as 'savants', locked in a world of technology, who just need the love of a good woman to help them break free.

And if you're insistent that geeks just aren't your style, consider the success of techno nerds Bill Gates (Microsoft) or Mark Zuckerberg (Facebook) and think again.

Internet dating could also work well for you, if you can get past the idea of it as catalogue shopping. Putting just the good-looking guys in your 'basket' on the basis that you can try them for one date then change your mind, like returning an ill-fitting pair of shoes to the store, is not what it's all about.

Instead, get a friend to pick out suitable online matches for you. If she's a really good friend she'll know your tastes but will also have your best interests at heart and choose potential partners who are more than just a pretty face.

Friends, in fact, can be a big factor in helping you find lasting love so don't dismiss their offers of help as interference, as they may know you better than you know yourself.

Also make a point of visiting exhibitions where new inventions are on show. It doesn't have to be dull and could include home design shows with cool high tech gizmos, and science museums with state of the art light shows, late-night openings, DJs and guest celebrity appearances.

Even the delivery guy dropping off your new digital music player could bring love straight to your door, as even the unlikeliest connection with technology is still one of the best clues that romantic electric sparks are about to light up your life.

2. Get Flying

Libra is an Air sign so you're in your element when you're

connected to things that get you out in the fresh air.

Simple pleasures can be the best so get flying, and start small with a kite. It can be a really sociable thing even on your own and offers a great opportunity to get someone (preferably male and cute) to help you get your kite off the ground.

Or if you're feeling bolder you can elevate your ambitions to hang-gliding, paragliding or actual gliding, letting the wind currents take you on an uplifting journey of discovery. Obviously make sure you're fit and able to experience these activities first. Or you could try something more serene, like a hot air balloon ride. Whether as a participant or spectator, each of these offers potential for meeting your future beloved.

In fact, people you may connect with strongly are likely to have an airborne link. This could be a flying instructor, someone in the Air Force or the pilot or a steward on your flight to a vacation destination.

You could, of course, meet these types randomly and that's quite possible and still fits in with the astrology, but why not give fate a hand and put yourself in places where your paths are more likely to cross? Air shows, for example, or even just picking up a friend from the airport. And if the situation coincides with your best love times, so much the better.

You could treat yourself to a helicopter ride over somewhere scenic near where you live or somewhere even more amazing like the Grand Canyon. You might click with the pilot, but it's more likely that you'll connect romantically with one of the other passengers.

If you're solo and on a flight, get into conversation with the guy sitting next to you, especially if you're a nervous flier and he's cute. It's not sad or crazy to ask him to hold your hand during take-off and if he's kind enough to oblige who knows where destiny might take you together.

You might fall for a plane-spotter or bird-watcher, or for a man whose hobby connects with airplanes. Don't dismiss such fascinations as, again, just being for unlovable geeks. One of the fittest men (in every sense) I've ever encountered was a Libran friend's partner who would run several miles to the gym and back each morning to work-out before going to work. He looked great and had a fantastic job, plus he even built their own house brick by brick. But he chose to spend his quiet moments flying model airplanes.

Remember that flying itself doesn't have to be the major part of the connection. So long as your feet are way above ground level you're on the right flight path. You could even meet your dream man in an elevator. Going up?

3. Get A Hobby

Dive into a hobby that you're obsessed with as nothing makes you more radiant than being consumed by a personal passion.

Your sign is more likely to meet someone away from a work situation rather than across the water-cooler or in the lunch queue in the staff café, so your interests and your romantic interests are best developed after working hours and at weekends.

If you truly want to meet someone special there's no point just staying in and watching TV, unless you connect with fans of a favorite cult or sci-fi program and go to meetings or conventions, which would certainly work for your sign.

It's all about joining forces with others, and where better to do that than on some kind of course? But choose wisely. Not just any old course. The kind of man who would be good for you to hook up with has eclectic interests.

He may be into astrology, which you too have an interest in since you're reading this book. Guys tend to be good at the technical stuff and often excel at the astronomy side of things, so you could trade strengths by offering to help with the intuitive and caring side of chart interpretation.

Not sure what to study? You could do worse than stick a pin

in a course guide and just go with whatever you pick at random. There's a real element of the unexpected when it comes to you and your future partner, so the less fixed or rigid you are the more likely it is that a space will open up for him to come into your life.

If you choose an art course, and you do have a fine artistic sense, make it one that encourages you to produce something quirky and innovative rather than traditionally beautiful. Or you may find you fall for someone on the course who paints or creates in a unique, individual way.

He might be teaching a computer skills or software course, or you might bump into him on his way to a class in electronics or on how to become an electrician.

And as Libra is also about balance you could even try learning circus skills. Meeting your love match while unicycling, juggling, or especially on a trapeze as that connects with your Air sign element, would certainly be a great 'how we met' story.

But it's not just about doing the course. After-class socializing is important for getting to know your fellow students better. Open up your social world and if no-one else mentions it, be the first to suggest going for a group coffee.

You'll get closer as friends too which could lead to something more as, for you, being friends with someone before you become lovers makes for a solid bond and a long-lasting relationship.

4. Get Rebellious

If you're a regular laid-back Libra it's possible that you do all you can to avoid confrontation and disturbing the peace. That's no bad thing as it makes the world a nicer, more harmonious place to live in.

Sometimes, though, you have to take a stand that might be controversial or might stir things up a little. You're a champion of fairness and equality, so where you see unfairness this is where you may need to step out of your role as Queen of Serene and go and rattle some cages.

If you've never felt moved to champion a particular cause, now's the time to get off the fence you sometimes feel more comfortable being perched upon. Because you're such a diplomat, your negotiating skills and calm approach could be invaluable to an organization that has its heart in the right place but can't get its act together to present a united and reasonable front.

It could be a political party, a human rights issue, saving a hospital from closure or campaigning to stop a superstore from opening up in your town. Find out what's going on locally and see where you can get involved.

Not only is this a wonderful thing to do to expand your experience as an individual, but you'll be helping your community, or even a different part of the world depending upon wherever the issue is that gets you all fired up.

And the even bigger plus is that you could meet a kindred spirit in the process. There's little that's more alluring to your sign than a man who's prepared to fight for justice and for a good cause. Remember though, that the man for you is the kind who'll help a cause or even a damsel in distress, but will expect that once she's back on her feet she'll be fighting alongside him!

This kind of controversy and friction could be just what you need, if you search deep inside yourself. Being polished and elegant is fine, and is something that your sign does with ease. You can be the most well-groomed rebel around if you choose, but it's what's in your heart and mind that counts, every time.

It's also about being brave enough to embrace change and do new things and meet unusual people, including potential partners. With other signs, it's easier to pinpoint what Mr. Right might do for a living or even what he might look like. For you, it's a case of expecting the unexpected. He might be completely unlike you'd pictured him but you'll recognize him by his strong social conscience that makes him get involved with putting the world to rights.

It might almost be easier to think of him as a masked superhero who one minute is fighting battles and righting wrongs as Batman and the next he's mild-mannered Bruce Wayne. That element of being two sides of the same coin will certainly appeal to your dual-natured sign, although other people might think you're like chalk and cheese. All that can be said for sure is when you find him you'll fit into each other's lives like the final missing piece of a jigsaw puzzle and it will feel just right.

So get out of your own way, think how you can help the world around you and you'll be helping yourself in a major way at the same time. The right man for you loves a woman who is happy in her own skin. Doing something that lets the real, caring, sharing you shine through means you're more likely to meet your soulmate as a result.

5. Get Wishing

This option is less about location and more of an avocation. How often have you simply wished for Mr. Right to turn up on your doorstep so you can begin the rest of your lives together? We've all been there and done that, usually without much success.

But here's a little secret that is just for Librans: You have more chance of wishing a man into your life than any of the other signs.

You've most likely heard of the law of attraction. If not, then the short version is that it's about sending the idea of your perfect life scenario out into the universe then just letting it happen. It's kind of wishing but with bells on. The plan is to imagine yourself into the kind of life and relationship you truly want.

For instance, if you tend to look on the bleak side and believe good things never come your way, that's what you're more likely to get.

We all send out vibrations and body language that others pick up on. If you think you're not good enough for someone, he'll think the same. If you feel you're not capable of being promoted at work, you may well continually get passed over for promotion.

So, bottom line, it's about positive thinking. Think yourself into what you want to be, who you want to be doing it with and where you'd like it all to happen.

Make an inspiration board, with pictures of everything you'd like in your life. Be specific. The kind of house: Is it by the sea, in the countryside or a penthouse apartment in the city? Put it on the board. The kind of car you want, the job you'd like to be doing? Put pictures of your dreams on the board and hang it where you can see it.

You can also add these images to your computer as screen-savers so the whole of your potential future life is flashing at you like a subliminal message of success.

Start to act as if you already have these things and you'll begin to vibrate on the same wavelength as them and eventually they may start to come your way. It can work, if you believe and your intentions don't waver, but at the same time don't obsess or stress about it.

You can add to and strengthen this by making wishes every new moon, so check your diary for the new moon dates each month or click onto www.orlilysen.com for monthly moon updates. And keep your wish list with you.

As your current intention is about attracting a soulmate, make a list of what you'd like in a partner and be specific. Although asking for Brad Pitt or George Clooney or for someone else's partner or husband is not the way to go, you can add some of the traits of men that you like to your list. More effective though is to imagine how you feel when you're with this man. Do you like yourself more? Are you happy, secure, more fun to be around? Think of it as less a shopping list for physical or financial attributes and more about that internal click you get when something feels just right.

Another way to do this, which will also connect you with others, is to join a meditation class. People from all walks of life seek the quietening of the mind that comes with meditation, so it's an ideal place for you to meet your future partner, plus it's been shown to help with health and stress issues too.

While you may not be encouraged to sit and meditate specifically on how to draw in your ideal man, promoting a sense of calmness, peace and love will go a long way towards raising your personal vibration, from one of longing for romance to one of openness and acceptance of what and who comes into your life. This in turn may open you up to attracting and meeting a new and different kind of man, as well as feeling better about life in general.

The key word here is vibration. The right man for you works on a frequency that, in order to find him, you need to tune into.

If you think this is nonsense and not for you, read this. A Libran friend who had lost touch with a man she later regretted breaking up with began to think about him every day, and set aside time to meditate about him. A year later their paths crossed, and the last time I saw her they were happily together and had a new baby boy. The power of positive thinking? Tuning in to the right frequency? You be the judge. You've nothing to lose and everything to gain by trying.

6. Get Alternative

If you're a typical Libra you tend to like doing things by the book, in the traditional way. That's all well and good, but where has it got you in the love stakes?

It's the old catch-22 situation, that doing what you always do just gets you the same results every time. The same kind of man, the same kind of experience. In fact it's a cycle that repeats itself so often that if it wasn't for the change of name you could almost have been dating the same guy each time.

So get out of that *Groundhog Day* rut. Break your routine, try something different, somewhere different with someone totally different from your usual type. And surprise yourself!

The first step is to change the location. Go to a music festival, camp out, forget your make-up and let your hair go wild. You'll feel free and no one will care what you look like as you, and everyone else, will be having way too good a time to notice. You might click with a DJ or a techno musician, especially one who's younger than you.

Try a Mind, Body and Spirit festival and go to different talks, especially about love and relationships. Your eyes will be opened to some new theories and ways of accepting yourself and how you relate that could rock your world.

These events attract fascinating people, including guys who are in tune with ideas and concepts that the kind of man you've normally gone for wouldn't necessarily understand. Your ideal partner thinks deeply, more openly and, in his way, more caringly than the more traditional macho men you might have dated so far. He could be the one offering energy healing, or taking photos of your aura.

Find yourself a free spirit and get in touch with your own sense of freedom. You could spend your life with a stuffed shirt who's all work and achievement, or with a man who'll drive for miles to take you for a moonlit walk, barefoot on the beach, just on impulse. It's possible to have a little of both but you need to make space for both in your life.

Take a walk on the wild side, moonlit or not, and see how you get on. Mr. Right could be waiting for you along that road less traveled.

7. Get Independent

Libra is the sign most connected to love and relationships so it's no wonder you're doing your best to look for love in all the right places. For you, it fills a deep desire to be part of someone or something bigger than you are and makes you feel in harmony with yourself as well as with the world around you.

But at times there's a sense of neediness that comes with this need to be one half of a couple that can repel rather than attract. Shocking as that may sound, take it as a green light to celebrate your independence and single status.

Being single can be great. You get to do what you want, when you want, without having to compromise, so whoever you eventually give that up for has got to be absolutely fabulous for it to be worth it.

The chances are you're already independent, up to a point, mainly because you've had to be. But where in life have you been too timid to branch out and try something new on your own?

Take a trip away by yourself, somewhere easy to start with, a beach holiday or a city break in your own country where there's loads to do and see. Then make it a little farther afield, a day trip abroad, for instance, where you may have the added element of dealing with an unknown language.

Have dinner on your own in a smart restaurant. Bring a book to read if that makes you feel more comfortable. Visit a museum or gallery by yourself and lose yourself in the beauty of the exhibits.

Go to a show or see a movie that you want to see. Sometimes it's quite a relief to do your own thing without having to round people up and deal with conflicts of opinion about who wants to see what and eat where. And do you always have to dissect the plot of the movie afterwards? Occasionally it's nicer just to have the story seep into your soul so you can savor it in peace.

If you haven't done this before, or at least not often, it may feel uncomfortable. That's the point. To get you doing things that you may have felt you can only do with someone else. You don't. You're in charge of your life. By pushing your boundaries and getting out of your comfort zone you'll realize that facing your fears, in your case a fear of being alone, only makes you stronger.

Enjoy the buzz and the challenge of trying something new and exciting without having to rely on others. Again this will send out a new sense of who you are, both to yourself and to people around you.

It's also easier to approach someone on their own than it is to invade the space of two or more people, even if they're just friends. So you're more likely to be approached and asked about an exhibit at a gallery, say, or for directions or even for your phone number if you're solo than if you seem joined at the hip to your best buddy.

Someone who's content with their own company and is enjoying the moment is extremely attractive, especially to the kind of man you're meant to have in your life. And the stronger you are emotionally the more likely you are to find each other.

It'll be spontaneous and seemingly random when you do meet, but it will be when you're in the right mindset and helped along by the stars aligning perfectly for you. So go book that weekend away for one... for now.

Location Checklist

A checklist is a handy way to focus your direction and pinpoint those places you need to add to your routine in order to help love along. This is not an exhaustive list but will give you the idea, and help you think of many more along similar lines. You could meet 'the one' at a:

- Mind, Body and Spirit festival
- Hang gliding session
- Air show
- Music festival
- Meditation center
- Modern art show
- Science Museum
- City break on your own

- Political rally
- Bird watching
- Elevator
- Local campaign
- Astrology course
- Internet dating
- Circus skills course
- Helicopter ride
- Air Force event
- IT store

When you've found your perfect partner, look back on this and smile at the memory of the time you met that cute alternative therapist in the elevator. He amazed you with his accurate reading of your aura, then persuaded you to help him campaign to protect some rare birds at a local park, and at the music festival held to raise funds you danced the night away in his arms. And the rest is history. Insert your own romantic 'how we met' story instead, of course.

Chapter 8

Where to Find Love if You're Scorpio

If you're Scorpio, the chances are you're bracing yourself for a list of dubious locations where your reputedly outrageous libido can help you get down and dirty.

While it's true you tend to send out a siren call to the universe that often unwittingly attracts those who'd rather bed you than wed you, there are sides to your astrological make-up that are deeply tender, vulnerable, spiritual and even charitable that, once developed, could bring an altogether different sort of mate your way.

It's all about location, location, location. When you're looking for romance you need to tune into the watery element of your sign to discover what sort of lover really floats your boat.

The other issue for you is that, while you're deeply intuitive and instinctive, you're also unfathomably suspicious so you must learn to trust your instincts but not automatically jump to the conclusion that potential lovers are out to do you wrong.

Past relationships may have seen you in the arms of guys who might have offered stability and material comforts but who restricted your personal growth and your movements, always wanting to know what you're doing, where you're going and even what you're thinking.

Since you're such a private person and it takes you a long time to fully trust anyone, even a close partner, such intrusions are not always welcome in your world. You're secretive, but not deceptive, which others often fail to comprehend. Your perceived lack of openness makes people assume you have a dark past but you might have nothing to hide at all, you're just naturally enigmatic.

And while you may have a thing about power and money, you

hate to be dominated by it as deep down you're ruled by your emotions rather than overstated displays of wealth.

The kind of man who would be ideal for you trusts you completely, as you will eventually trust him. He's as intuitive as you are insightful so there's absolute transparency in your partnership. There has to be, as if not he'd soon sense it and you'd soon unearth any underhandedness on his part, so honesty and openness are your only options.

He's creative, spiritual, understanding and seems to merge with your soul as well as your mind. This guy also has a healing effect on some of the self-doubts you often seem to be plagued with.

He's out there and ready for you. All you need to do now is find him. Here's how.

1. Get Physical

Being in tune with your body helps you connect with everything around you at a deeper level, and clears your very sensitive mind. So the healthier your body is the better you'll feel, and feeling good about yourself is a major factor in the successful pursuit of romance.

Slogging away at the gym is not ideal as you tend to work-out as if it's some kind of punishment. Instead head to the beach as being near water is incredibly beneficial for you. You could swim, or jog by the water's edge or, even better, get fit as you clean up a beach or a river walk because your sign is all about transforming the grubbier side of life, but in a good way.

A relationship is being part of a team so you want to see how your potential Significant Other interacts not just with you but with anyone else you encounter so, though you often prefer to fly solo, in this case some kind of group effort is ideal. Plus you'll be outdoors, being active and meeting like-minded others. Check the internet for local groups and organizations that may need volunteers for a river or beach clean-up, for an altogether different way of getting down and dirty.

Scuba diving is another sportier option to try as trust is often an issue with you and on a diving course you'll pair up with a dive buddy who has to have your back at all times and vice versa. This is a great learning curve too as you can't just up and go at the first sign of trouble or discord.

If you like the idea of getting fit and learning a skill at the same time, training to be a pool or beach lifeguard would also be perfect for you as you have a knack of being incredibly cool and calm in a crisis. You might also find that you click with a guy who's a lifeguard, as rescue is a strong theme in your love-life.

Better yet, try wild swimming. This involves exploring lakes and natural pools in beautiful settings. Not only will it tap into the part of you that's unconventional and likes a challenge, it's an almost meditative exercise as it gets you back to nature in the raw and attracts the kind of free-spirited man who you'll want to bond with for life. Again, check online for wild swimming sites and groups near you, or if you're planning a vacation consider taking a dip in places like the stunning and naturally thermal Blue Lagoon in Iceland.

Canoeing, kayaking or joining a rowing club would also work to help you make a romantic connection and, if you really aren't up to being quite so physical, groups like these always need people to organize events, handle admin and be generally supportive. So put whatever skills you already have to use, learn some new ones and network, as it's the location as much as what you do there that puts you in the right place for love.

With that in mind, you could meet someone at your local pool, while doing aqua aerobics or even learning synchronized swimming, but you could just as easily meet him over a coffee at the pool-side café. Finding a guy who's true soulmate material at last could be simpler than you imagined.

2. Get Creative

You're more creative than you may realize, with the potential to become truly absorbed by (to the point of being obsessed with) any artistic activity that captures your imagination. It's a fantastic way to lose yourself and forget to be self-consciousness as you become completely immersed in doing the thing that nurtures your soul as well as your mind.

Photography is a fabulous outlet for you. Did you ever really read the instructions on that digital camera you got for Christmas? Exactly. So you have the perfect reason to learn on a course and talk to the hot guy with the Hasselblad who will be delighted to share his knowledge with you and, who knows, maybe more.

The creative results don't have to be technically perfect but your sign's skill is in capturing something deeper than first meets the eye.

Likewise, painting not only allows you to create something visually alluring it also helps you express the darker places in your psyche as art of any sort is highly therapeutic for you. Watercolor painting may suit you best, or try a life drawing class as you have a gift for appreciating the naked body whether it's conventionally beautiful or not.

However you choose to express yourself you can be sure that your output will fascinate those around you and be an instant, if sometimes controversial, talking point. You're particularly drawn to and easily attract sensitive types who love to look at the real meaning behind things, so you could hook up with a photographer or photography tutor, or an art therapist.

You could also find love with someone who rescues unwanted or unloved *objects d'art*. He could be an antiques dealer but he's more likely to run a junk shop or thrift store. Either way he could be the man for you as recycling or upcycling (making something desirable out of pre-owned objects) is another creative area for you to explore, as your sign has a flair for transforming things that other people may have rejected as worthless. In the past that may have included some of the men in your life too, but not any more!

Bring a watery theme to your projects if you want to catch the eye of an art lover who could love you as well as your work. Or book a vacation where you'll learn to paint by the sea because you could find Mr. Right setting up an easel beside you.

If you really don't feel that the creative muse is going to inspire you to make something of your own, don't despair. If you've ever said: "I don't know anything about art but I know what I like" then visit a gallery or two and discover some things you do like.

Some national galleries have late open nights and offer wine and music too, so you're practically guaranteed to encounter someone on your wavelength. Or support a local gallery and get invited to private views where you could hit it off with the gallery owner.

If you've never considered doing anything along these lines before, that's the very reason to try it now. And you may only need to do it once if it ties in with your best love days, as it's by doing something different that you can break the cycle of disappointing romance.

3. Get Dancing

Anywhere you can dance is especially good for you when it comes to finding love. The way someone dances reveals a lot about their real personality, and you're a master of reading body language so you'll very quickly know whether or not you're with someone whose rhythms are in time and in tune with your own.

Tango, that dark and passionate expression of the thin line between love and hate, is a perfect way to express your deeper feelings and to get close to someone who's not afraid to express himself creatively too.

The more body contact the better for your sensual sign, but

combining fitness with dance is another option too as you're often intrigued by unconventional ways to keep healthy. Try a Five Rhythms class, a free-style dance session that helps you express how you feel to music, individually, paired up or as a group. It's not for the faint-hearted but can be very liberating and increases self-confidence which is also pretty sexy. And the possibility of connecting with someone who's in touch with his emotions, who loves to dance and is, as a result, fit and desirable too will appeal to your own five senses in a major way.

You don't have to limit yourself to organized sessions or dance courses. It could be as simple as finding love with a single dad who likes your moves as you do the actions to 'The Wheels on the Bus' at his child's party.

Getting your groove on at a music festival or gig could also attract compliments and an admirer, especially if it's happening by a lakeside or in a 'repurposed' church. Even the UK's Glastonbury Festival with its legendary rain-soaked terrain could turn out to be the right location for love.

And if you truly don't like the idea of busting a move, you could instead find love beside the dancing fountains at the Bellagio Hotel in Las Vegas, or the Magic Fountain in Barcelona, or by one of the biggest dancing fountains in the world in front of the tallest building in the world, the Burj Khalifa in Dubai. It may sound random, but connecting your sign's watery element to dance creates a double link for love.

You could even encounter love at a performance of *Swan Lake*. A Scorpio friend of mine went to see a production of the all-male version of this ballet, spotted her ideal man in the foyer on the way in (a complete stranger), then found out she was sitting next to him during the performance. And unlike the tale in the ballet, her love story with him ended happily ever after.

4. Get Spiritual

You're often more drawn than you care to admit to the spiritual side of life.

Faith and beliefs aside, we're talking about location, and as numerous churches are now being converted into community centers or concert halls, when you're looking for love there's a very strong chance of you finding romance within those (formerly or currently) sacred spaces.

If you love to sing, think about joining a church choir as music tends to soothe your sometimes troubled soul. Singing groups unconnected to religion also often meet in sanctified buildings as the acoustics are divine. Uplifting harmonies, especially in dark, candlelit surroundings with ornate interiors and incense are truly magical for you, and with your link to things that are deep and low, a bass baritone guy could totally steal your heart.

Or a venue that offers gospel singing to join in with or simply to listen to may be more in tune with your tastes and help you connect with the man you're meant to be with.

Going to or helping out at a church fund-raiser could bring you closer to your Mr. Right. He could be manning the refreshments stand, or you could bump into him while you're rummaging through pre-owned items with good upcycling potential. He might even be a man of the cloth which would be a surprisingly good match for your sign.

On a different spiritual plane, learning yoga is another option that may work for you romantically. It's a beautiful way to unwind your mind while twisting your body into pretzel shapes. If you delve into its mysteries as deeply as you usually do with things once your interest in piqued you'll find that physically fit and spiritually-attuned guys tend to go for the more power-driven versions, like Ashtanga yoga. Again, it's not vital to take on board yoga's spiritual aspects if that's not your style, you'll still benefit from an holistic mind, body and soul workout.

You might instead fall for someone who has mediumship skills at a spiritualist church, which would suit your sign's fascination for all things other-worldly. Or he could be a dream interpreter so a psychic fair could put you in touch with the man whose future is intertwined with yours.

It could be as simple as a close encounter with your kindred spirit at a Mind, Body and Spirit book store and with your instincts about karma and destiny on high alert on your best love days, you'll know when you've met 'the one'.

5. Get Healing

As a Scorpio you can be intensely private at times, preferring to keep yourself to yourself, so it may help you to have a specific reason to connect with other people.

One sure way is to be able to offer some kind of therapy. Whatever you give out you get back in kind, so if you're making others feel good you're bound to feel better than ever too.

If there's a therapeutic treatment you've experienced and enjoyed, or would like to, think about learning how to do it yourself. Remember this is about location and connections, so it's not necessarily the person you're doing it to or having it done by, although that could work, but more about where it's taking place which could bring a potential partner into your life. You could meet someone on a course or even encounter your future partner in the waiting room if you've arrived early for a treatment you've booked as a personal treat.

Therapies you'd find in a spa (as again that water element is all-important) are the real winners for you. Your sign is often extremely tactile as well as super-sensitive so you're likely to have a sixth sense about what feels good in a massage, what pressure to use and even where the real healing needs to be taking place, so you might consider learning or having energy work like reiki.

Or you could meet a kindred spirit on a detox break as cleansing the body helps you ditch the emotional baggage you often carry around, and leaves you open to new and less toxic romance.

Foot care therapies especially resonate with you. As your sign has a tendency to wear sexy high heels you could benefit from a soothing treatment yourself, one that could lead to a romantic connection with a cute chiropodist or a reflexologist.

And with your sign's often mesmerizing voice and magnetic eyes, don't rule out trying out or taking a course in hypnotherapy. You might even fall under the romantic spell of a stage hypnotist.

If alternative therapies are not your thing, you could always help out at your local hospital. Giving your time to care for others is more important for you than you may realize. And volunteering at a children's ward may be especially good for you as you're surprisingly compassionate when it comes to those less fortunate than yourself, being more in touch with your own damaged or wounded inner child than most.

While you're giving selflessly you may be attracting the eye and potentially the admiration of doctors, health workers, or friends or family visiting relatives. The beauty of doing this is that you could find you get out of your own way enough to forget that you're on a mission to find Mr. Right, which is precisely when he'll enter your life.

And if you're seeking emotional healing yourself, one of the best ways for you to do this is to go on a retreat, ideally in a sanctuary or an ancient monastery, as this taps into your spiritual side too. You could find inner peace as you learn to relax and open up, but it's also where you could find the man of your dreams who may be on a similar quest.

6. Get Drinking

Yours is one of the few signs who may genuinely meet your match over that old dating standby, going out for a drink. Avoid the obvious choice of hanging out at a bar and choose a wine-tasting session or beer festival instead. You'll encounter guys who are experts in their field who'll be more than happy to enlighten you about their favorite subject. And you could study to become an expert yourself.

There is a slight warning here about over-indulging, as both you and the people you're attracted to are likely to have addictive personalities.

At its most extreme you could meet your partner in an AA meeting or rehab center as you do have a tendency to go for vulnerable types who you feel need to be saved.

If there's a chance that you've been down that path before and as this book is all about getting you out of recurring habits and onto your true path of love, recognize the signs and think about making your local coffee bar rather than the nearest wine bar your favorite hang-out. You could fall for a barista or for the guy who likes his coffee the same weird way you do.

The thing to remember is that it's not necessarily all about the activity, but about where it's taking place. So it could be the guy behind the juice bar counter at the yoga center (which also taps into your 'Get Healing' option) who turns out to be Mr. Right if the stars are in the right place at the right time to make love happen.

Or he could be someone who reads your fortune in the tea leaves at a psychic fair (see 'Get Spiritual' too). And if you can double up your location options this way, you're doubling up your chances of meeting your soulmate too.

7. Get Fishing

In some way, shape or form, fish may be part of your quest to find your true love. Because the sign of Pisces rules your romance zone, things connected to that aquatic symbol have a strong influence over your romantic destiny.

It could be as simple as falling for a fishmonger, tying the knot with a trawler man or hooking up with the guy in the fishing tackle shop where you've been sent by a lazy guy friend to buy bait.

He might pilot a lifeboat, though an invitation to dine at the captain's table on a cruise ship is more likely to lead to love, especially if seafood is on the menu.

Options could also include a romantic encounter at an aquarium, love at first sight with someone you've bought a fish tank from via a small ad, or sitting in a bar called 'Neptune' and locking eyes with someone across the room.

Movies are another indication that you're heading in the right direction for romance. It doesn't have to involve a marathon session of all the *Jaws* movies, instead you could find love with a guy taking his nephews to a showing of *Finding Nemo*.

The man for you could have a dolphin tattoo, not strictly a fish but still in the same watery ballpark, or he might be wearing a piece of jewelry shaped like a fish.

You could meet him in an elegant fish restaurant on the beach in Bali or he could be the man serving you salty fish and chips wrapped in newspaper in the UK.

It may seem random but if you want to increase your chances of finding the right partner be aware of the little signs and omens that the universe sends you, especially when the planets are connecting in your favor.

Make a note of your best love dates so you can be in the right place at the right time. Turning a different corner and taking a chance on something that might appear crazy at first could make a world of difference to your love life.

Location Checklist

A checklist is a handy way to focus your direction and pinpoint those places you need to add to your routine in order to help love along. This is not an exhaustive list but will give you the idea, and help you think of many more along similar lines. You could meet 'the one' at a:

- Movie
- Juice bar

- Fishing trip
- Singing group
- Scuba diving
- Wild swimming
- Beach clean-up
- River walk
- Psychic fair
- Wine tasting
- Hospital
- Reflexology center
- Spa
- Yoga center
- Tango class
- Dance at a church hall
- Concert in a cathedral
- Taking photos

When you've found your perfect partner, look back on this and smile at the memory of the time your dog swam out of his depth at the lake in the park and how Mr. Right, who was organizing a lake-side clean-up nearby, rowed out to rescue him. Having saved your dog, he invited you to a tango night at a cool, converted chapel, and as the sultry music played you danced and seemed to merge together as one. And the rest is history. Insert your own romantic 'how we met' story instead, of course.

Chapter 9

Where to Find Love if You're Sagittarius

You're the adventurer of the zodiac, even if you're simply an armchair traveler, visiting exotic locations in your imagination.

You like to think big, ponder life's big questions and make oversized plans, because even if you only achieve a fraction of what you'd like to do in life it's better than having no plans, schemes and dreams to look forward to.

It's the same with love. When you're in love you're so full of passion that the object of your desire feels your emotions like a force of nature. But when you want your freedom, as you often do, you can be off and running before anyone even knows you're gone. You're an all or nothing kind of gal, who has to be true to herself and her beliefs.

So the thing you need to bear in mind if you want love to work is to find someone who's as passionate as you but who, like you, values space to do his own thing so that neither of you feels restricted or hemmed in.

You also need stimulation, certainly of the intellectual kind, to keep things interesting for you. Previously you may have gone for guys who might have made you think, but they've tended to have all the ideas just not the drive you like to get things moving.

You're a thinker too but you're also a doer, often rushing into your latest scheme without fully checking all the details. But that element of risk, the unknown and the adventure, are what spell fun for you.

So someone who can not only get the party started but keep it going is more your style. A man who's as mentally and even physically dynamic as you can be will present you with the kind of challenge you adore, and you'll exhaust each other in such a good way that you'll both be coming back for more of the same.

You have your gentler moments too when you can be very spiritual, loving to share your knowledge or to be an eternal student always wanting to find out more.

Your home might be full of books and magazines, plus you're very aware of the media so you'll have access to every TV channel available as you love to keep informed.

You can also be a tad blunt without meaning to hurt or offend, as to you it's simply being honest and truthful, qualities you admire and expect in others. So someone who can take your no-frills comments in his stride is going to stay the course far better than a more sensitive type.

As far as you're concerned, life is to be enjoyed, not just endured. And as one of your sign's philosophies is 'the more the merrier' life will be even better with two of you on the journey together. All you have to do now is find him, so here's how and where.

1. Get Creative

If you want to meet someone on your wavelength, get in touch with your creative side. We're not talking about painting water-colors. Try metalwork. There's a strong chance that you'll have real ability with this art form and, while there are excellent female blacksmiths around, metalwork courses tend to attract a higher percentage of guys which is another good reason for you to consider taking it up.

Don't get this confused with shoeing horses, that's what farriers do, although with your sign's symbol incorporating the half human, half horse centaur that's appropriately enough another option you might want to consider if you have an affinity with horses, as many Sagittarians do.

Working with fire can be very therapeutic for you and making decorative metalwork is an unusual pastime so you'll have a fantastic conversation starter. And if you get really good at it you can sell your creations, and that too can open up a whole new social scene as you set up shop at craft fairs or high-end design festivals.

You like playing with fire in your relationships too, so this is a subliminal way of learning how to control the flames rather than let them run wild and consume you as they sometimes do in the heat of passion.

However, if you really don't feel drawn to the idea of welding things in a decorative way, you could apply the principles more practically on a car maintenance course or a plumbing course, either of which will also put you in touch with guys who'll be sure to want to impress and help you, even though you're smart enough not to need their assistance. Your sign has a special connection with education and knowledge, so the hot tutor could be the one to capture your heart.

You can always take this down to an even smaller scale and learn to create jewelry, as manipulating silver and gold into beautiful creations alongside manly silversmiths may be more your thing.

Another option is to study some of the more fiery elements of cuisine. Learn to make a perfect crème brûlée complete with blowtorch skills, or go on a course to make hot and spicy meals. Do this for your own pleasure and to increase your knowledge and skill but be aware also that all things dramatic or laced with an element of bravado are what guys who are suitable for you tend to favor, so you're more likely to encounter a possible partner in a more masculine environment than on a cake-making course.

And remember that the man you fall for doesn't have to be creative, although he might be. It's all about the location and putting yourself in the right kind of place at the right time, to meet the right guy no matter how odd or random it may seem. Link it with your best love days and you're practically guaranteed to connect.

2. Get Barbecuing

Parties are a great way to meet people, that's obvious, but for you one type of social get-together is more likely to win you your Mr. Right than any other.

Barbecues are the perfect spring or summer option for catching up with old friends and being introduced to some new ones too. Get invited to any barbecue you hear of, and consider throwing one of your own where the invitation says to bring a bottle and preferably a spare man as well.

You're not known for being subtle, and sometimes being blunt like this actually works better than a whole heap of gentle hints that may go unnoticed. So long as you get your message across with your legendary sense of humor no one could possibly take offense. And besides, you may be making matches for other single friends into the bargain.

Consider a beach barbecue or two as well, so long as you're kind to the environment while you're about it. You're often at your best in the great outdoors, as potential admirers won't fail to notice.

You also have other wonderful options for fiery gatherings. Bonfire Night in the UK, Independence Day in the US, and Oz has Australia Day. None is complete without fireworks and more food cooked al fresco, the kind of thing that appeals to your sense of adventure and being out in the elements.

But why stick with days 'set in stone'? Do it whenever you like, including fall and winter. Breaking with convention is part of your nature so holding your own random event just for the joy of it is almost to be expected of you. It would also be a fabulous way to celebrate your birthday.

Keep an eye on the bonfire though, if you have one, as while it is a good idea for your sign to hook up with a fireman, burning your home down in the pursuit of romance is not.

Look out for other events where bonfires or fireworks are part of the activities too. New Year firework displays are ideal. The kind of man for you likes to be first at everything he does, so welcoming in the first day of the New Year with fiery celebrations is a good place to find him. Better still, and this could also tie in with your sign's legendary wanderlust, is to greet the New Year in one of the first countries to welcome it in, so you could potentially meet your match in New Zealand.

You don't have to travel far, though. Just remember that food and fire are key ingredients in your quest for love. So you could meet your soulmate at a local pizza parlor, but do choose one where they use wood fired ovens.

3. Get Active

You may already be a pretty active person if you're typical of your sign. This doesn't necessarily mean you go to the gym, as just being out in the fresh air or walking the dog is much more your style.

If you like the idea of getting fitter think about trying military style boot camp training. You'll be outside enjoying nature and though it sounds tough you won't be pushed beyond your limits (even though your sign doesn't always know its limits) as the companies running these events want you to come back for more, not run you into the ground.

The most unlikely people become addicted to this style of training, including one stylish Sagittarius fashion magazine editor I know who adores getting wet and muddy, exhilarated and toned all at the same time. Plus she swears it's a great way to meet men who are fit, in every sense of the word.

If this doesn't appeal, consider taking up karate, judo or kickboxing. Still too fierce? Gentler Tai Chi, based on ancient Chinese warrior techniques, may fit the bill and also attracts more spiritually-minded men.

You could also try a self-defense class which, although it may well be with other women, may have a guy instructor you might just hit it off with, in the nicest way.

Another possibility is to make fitness fun by joining in a paint-balling session or heading to the archery range, which is perfect for your sign, to see if you can score a bull's-eye as well as scoring with one of your fellow archers.

Shooting practice at a rifle range, clay pigeon shooting or supervised target practice with a pistol are also great things to do to improve your hand to eye co-ordination and to meet a potential soulmate. It's not about killing things, let's be clear, it's about the thrill of hitting the target, and the intense concentration and power that goes with that can be very sexy indeed.

And if you really, truly can't face being so active you could glam up for a night out at a boxing match, or meet your own perfect man watching Formula One racing or a sports game on the big screen at your local watering hole. You can be one of the guys but still be all woman.

4. Get into Uniform

This isn't about you dressing up saucily to seduce someone, in fact it's the complete opposite as men in uniform are the types you should seek out for a long-term romance.

Every man looks fabulous in uniform but for you there's a special resonance with men who have any kind of military background, especially those who deal with weaponry or firearms.

This may be at odds with your personal beliefs as Sagittarians are usually philosophers rather than fighters, but there can be an attraction if you open your heart and mind to the possibility.

At worst you can have some hot debates about your completely different viewpoints, which can turn into 'conflict flirting', that point when you're arguing just to heighten the sexual tension before passion takes over.

If you don't happen to live near an Air Force or Army base, or near a port where the Navy might come into town, put yourself in the line of fire (though not literally) by going to military reviews, try an online dating site that specializes in finding uniformed partners, or think about becoming the penpal of someone on the frontline as overseas connections and long distance romances are not uncommon for your sign. Even historical re-enactment societies with their muskets and swords could be where you find your knight in shining armor.

This is about thinking outside the box too. Men in uniform aren't just in the militia. Doctors and dentists wield knives and wear white coats or green scrubs during operations. Acupuncturists often wear medical coats, and chefs wear uniforms when they're chopping up vegetables and carving meat. It should be easy enough to get to know a chef, especially if you eat out regularly at a place where the food is as divine as the man making it. You could always ask to see the chef to give him your compliments (and your phone number).

And it's not just about the uniform, it's about what they do in it. So fireman? Yes. Ticket inspector? Could be. Construction worker, nope, but butcher? Potentially yes again. Hairdressers, often clad in uniform black, count too thanks to their scissor-wielding skills.

Even a circus fire-eater or sword-swallower could fit the bill, and while you may not have envisaged the man of your dreams working in a circus you're broad-minded enough and have a sense of humor that's well developed enough to see past the craziness and into his heart to find love.

5. Get Red-dy

Love can come into your life in ways that you would least expect. By using the options suggested for you here, you should be aware by now that there are tell-tale signs that you're in the right place at the right time, you just have to be alert to them.

In your case, the color red may have particular significance for you when it comes to finding romance.

You could be at a red traffic light and find that your ideal man is in the scarlet sports car in the next lane. Or you might be giving blood at the Red Cross, a triple whammy if ever there was one as you're got the color red and the connection with someone who may be wearing a uniform and using a sharp instrument as he goes about his work.

Alternatively he could be your motor mechanic wearing red overalls or a businessman looking dapper with a red tie, or the guy you've liked from a distance but have not been sure why until one day he turns up on a motorbike, sporting red leathers, and you're smitten. This isn't saying that you'll fall for every or any man wearing a hint of red, but if you're feeling the love vibes and the timing is right, this could be a sign to clinch the deal.

It's one of those things that sounds quite bizarre, but sometimes you just have to trust the astrology.

Since your sign clicks with travel, you might meet your match on a trip to Australia's Red Center, home of the fabulous and mystical Ayers Rock (Uluru). This would work better than the Red Sea or even the Red River, simply because it is actually red, and located in hot and dry terrain. So the Red Fort in Delhi with its red sandstone walls could work too if you happen to be traveling that way, but don't rule out even the most tenuous connections with the color, as a local bar, restaurant or café with 'red' in its name ('The Red Fort' Indian restaurant, for instance) could also be the right place to meet your future soulmate.

Closer to home, look for sports events where the team wears red. Your potential soulmate may follow this team or play sport himself, which could account for the scar on his head or face (you may have to look hard to find it). He might even have red hair.

And if you want to increase your chances of your love match finding you instead of you having to do all the work, consider investing in a few red items of clothing or sexy scarlet high heels yourself to help move things along.

6. Get Exploring

Freedom means a lot to you. You don't like being restricted at work or personally and will try your utmost to do things your own way because that's how you express yourself and your ideas best.

Not everyone understands that, and if your past relationships have shuddered to a halt through lack of communication or over-possessiveness on your other half's part, you need to put yourself in the path of someone who will love you for who you are and what you are, not who they want you to be.

So tap into your crusading spirit and be adventurous. Try something different, and in particular travel somewhere different to increase your chances of finding the right man for you. Ideally it should be a first, not just a first for you but perhaps the first time a travel company has gone to a particular country or run a particular event.

But where in the world is unexplored? There aren't that many places left, it seems, but click on adventure company websites and see what new things they have to offer.

Burma, closed to the rest of the world for a long time, recently re-opened its doors to foreign visitors. And countries such as Tibet, Bhutan and Nepal where it's possible to make pilgrimages are potentially the kinds of destinations to add to your to-do list, as you're quite a spiritual soul on the quiet.

And taking part in an overseas aid campaign may appeal to both your spiritual side and your desire for justice for all, and could be the perfect environment to locate the right kind of man for you.

You might consider volunteering whatever skills you have to offer in the event of an international disaster like a volcanic eruption or earthquake. This might sound an extreme way to meet a guy but by getting out of your own way and forgetting your need for a partner, you could actually find yourself working alongside him. And in times of crisis bonding is likely to occur deeper and quicker than in everyday life. Again, though, don't put yourself in harm's way just to find a man.

Organizations such as Voluntary Service Overseas might inspire you as they want volunteers with regular talents including office skills or teaching ability rather than daredevil stuff. This means you get to do what you already know how to do but in another environment that stretches your abilities because of the different challenges in a foreign and usually less developed country. So you would be a pioneer, adventurer and crusader of sorts if you decided to give this a try, and you may meet the kind of free-spirited, deep thinking, courageous and dedicated man you deserve, who could make you happy for life.

7. Get Smiling

Your sign's sense of humor and ability to look on the bright side of life is a real asset, and one you should definitely make the most of.

First of all, though, how's your smile looking? If your pearly whites aren't quite pearly or so white, it's time to get to the dentist.

Luckily for you the dentist's surgery is a possible place for romance for your sign. It sounds unlikely that anyone could ever hook up with their dentist with so much going on to obstruct conversation but you'd be surprised. Somehow over the course of two or three visits to my own dentist, when all I recall doing was nodding and trying to stretch my numbed-by-injection face into a smile at his jokes, he asked me out.

He wasn't meant for me, but you are a sexy Sagittarius so someone you meet while you're having a cleanse and polish could keep you smiling for a long time to come. It could even be another patient you encounter in the waiting room so you might want to book your appointments around your best love dates to make sure your mouth is supremely kissable.

Also, take the opportunity to go to places where your sense of humor is on show. Cutting-edge comedy clubs can be great for meeting guys, and even if you don't strike it lucky at first you'll come out feeling great through shared laughter.

And if you want to get noticed think about having a go at stand-up comedy yourself. You're likely to excel at this, especially if your routine is in a storytelling style or in the form of a comedy philosophy session. Your combative yet cute put-downs to hecklers could win you considerable admiration from someone hot who likes a fiery gal who speaks her mind.

Location Checklist

A checklist is a handy way to focus your direction and pinpoint those places you need to add to your routine in order to help love along. This is not an exhaustive list but will give you some ideas, and help you to think of many more along similar lines. You could meet 'the one' at a:

- Circus
- Boxing match
- Barbecue
- Bonfire party
- Karate course
- Military parade
- Pizza restaurant
- Voluntary Service Overseas posting
- Jewelry making course
- Acupuncture clinic
- Comedy club
- Metalwork course
- Adventure vacation
- Ayers Rock
- Boot camp fitness course
- Hairdressers
- Dentist

- Indian restaurant

When you've found your perfect partner, look back on this and smile at the memory of the time you met that cute fireman with the great sense of humor and ridiculous pick up lines. He asked you out to the opening night of a new comedy club, followed by a beach barbecue, where you sat together holding hands under a star-filled sky. And the rest is history. Insert your own romantic 'how we met' story instead, of course.

Chapter 10

Where to Find Love if You're Capricorn

Capricorn often has a bad rap as being the overly sensible and serious sign of the zodiac, but that's far from the truth as you know very well, though you often don't attempt to dispel the myth.

In a way you kind of like your designated role and it's only yourself that you tend to put restrictions upon, not other people.

It's your ruling planet Saturn that makes you inclined to step away from spontaneity and craziness, as your default setting is to remain in control and dignified at all times. But this planet also makes you very determined to succeed in other areas of your life, so now's the time to put that incredible tenacity you possess towards laying the foundations for a successful relationship.

Two things may have tripped you up you in the past. Firstly, you don't like to rush into things. There's nothing wrong with that but sometimes you hold back to the point where the moment has gone.

Secondly, you may need to relax your need for control and to count the cost of everything. A little luxury and comfort is something to which you're more than entitled. Think of it as an investment in yourself and your future rather than as a frivolity and you'll be in the right mindset to let yourself go and love the experience, and the man that comes with it. And remember that in order to draw your ideal man towards you, you need to speculate to accumulate.

Previously you may have been attracted to soft, gentle types who tend to bend to your will. You like and, in fact, usually excel in a leadership role but a successful love partnership is all about equality. Someone has to take the lead at times but that should be something that's taken in turns not assumed as a right, even if you do think you can do things better than anyone else.

Instead, set your sights on someone who challenges you. The right man for you wants stability and security as much, if not more, than you do but for him that includes enjoying what his money can buy as well as keeping some aside for a comfortable old age. He'll invest in quality, not quantity, and will relish good food, beautiful surroundings and the very best he can afford. He's also likely to be a very sensual guy so rather than stick with your sometimes spartan and practical existence, prepare to let him indulge you in a whole world of tactile treats.

Love is a personal pleasure and it's not to be skimped on. If you think you don't deserve it or can't afford it, that's what the universe will give you: A big fat zero. Believe that you have a right to happiness and fulfillment and that will come your way instead.

You're seeking long-term stability rather than fleeting passion and you can have it. Why? Because you're worth it, and here's where you're likely to find it.

1. Get Into The Garden

Take time out from your busy schedule to smell the roses. You may have a green thumb or you might be more likely to unwittingly murder plants but either way, if you want to cultivate a relationship that's going to take root and blossom, getting in touch with nature is the way to go.

Get yourself to a garden center. They're more happening places than you may realize if you're not into plants, with coffee shops and even non-gardening stuff to browse through and buy too.

Anywhere that nature has a big say in things is a good place for you to find love. If you adore flowers and plants this will be a dream mission for you to accomplish, but if not think about visiting well-established and prestigious horticultural shows where there are designer gardens and celebrity events, which may just make you change your mind. You may get some great ideas for a very practical vegetable patch of your own, which could link you to the man of your dreams.

If gardening truly isn't ever going to be your thing, start taking walks in the countryside. You could join a walking association where the rambles often end in a relaxed and sociable meal. Or borrow a friend's dog to walk as pets are great conversation starters.

You could even go on a walking vacation as it's not only one of the best forms of exercise you can do, but you'll get to see different parts of the world up close and personal, and meet great people of all ages and backgrounds too.

The main point here is to be outside amongst greenery and wildlife, in the fresh air, not cooped up indoors. Your sign has a tendency towards being a workaholic and you often find it easier to be shackled to your desk until all hours than to do things simply for pleasure and good health. This combines both, with the added bonus of helping you to potentially find a partner in the process.

Your sign's element is Earth, and there is an earthy side to you that you often neglect or even repress, so be on the lookout for a sexy gardener or a rugged farmer tending to his herd of cows while you're out communing with nature. He could very well be your Mr. Right.

2. Get Arty

When you think of art, you're most likely considering some kind of investment rather than producing some artwork of your own.

While it's true you have an eye for things you can turn into a profit and you tend to have an affinity with antiques, if you can bear to break out of your comfort zone you could meet your match at a jewelry-making workshop, a fine art class or sculpture course, and discover a new skill at the same time.

If you do strike up a relationship, it's more likely to be with an older, more experienced tutor as you tend to respect and admire those with authority. Or it could be a younger, impossibly talented artist that you fall for as you're not only passionate about people who do their thing to the very best of their abilities, but your sign often attracts partners who are very different from you in age.

If creating art of your own isn't really for you then consider hanging out with art dealers, gallery owners and the type of man who frequents auction houses or even posh junk shops or thrift stores, as there's a strong chance that one of these guys could become an extremely valuable addition to your life.

It may pay you to take a course in art appreciation and antiques too if you don't already know about these areas, especially if you've marveled at the prices quoted on relics found in the attic on TV antiques shows. You like to be the best at whatever you do and show expertise and knowledge, so you could meet someone as you learn, or if you develop a reputation for knowing your stuff you may be surprised at who may come your way to ask for your opinion or a valuation.

You could even start to specialize and run an antiques business or stall of your own, which multi-tasks in that it gets you out and about and meeting new people and brings you an income at the same time.

You're more likely to succeed, both business-wise and in the quest for love, if you sell or buy beautiful things. Go out of your way to select exquisite paintings, soft old leather chairs, rich textiles and classic watches for example, as the very man you want and need in your life will be attracted to these kinds of things and so, in theory, to the kind of woman who's selling them. Alternatively, he could be the one selling these retro-chic items so keep an eye out for him.

Another related area is interior design. Whether or not you have an eye for home decorating, it's something that has to be done at some stage wherever you live, and you could meet your dream man in the heritage paints department at your local DIY store. Seriously, you won't find him in the bargain or cut-price aisles. Or he'll be at a reclamation center that sells architectural antiques, salvaged items and curiosities. He loves his home, its treasures and his home comforts.

Make sure you splash out on a few home luxuries for yourself too, adding a touch of sensuality to your life to give you a taste of even more that's still to come. Start with your home and let that filter through to your personal style and the energy you give out. Guys will pick up on that subtle hint of extra warmth about you and you'll be more approachable without realizing why. It's not magic but it works like magic, so there's even more reason to bring a little artfulness into your life.

3. Get Musical

It's said that music is the food of love. But when was the last time you bought a new CD or went to a gig? Your mission, then, is to put more musical pleasure into your life and in doing so meet your ideal man.

You don't have to spend a fortune in the process, although if you want to meet a top man sometimes you have to pay top dollar to circulate in the kind of places that present the right kind of music where he might be found.

You can be quite traditional in your tastes so if you like opera and classical music then once in a while dress up and book seats in a box. You'll certainly be on show and may even be approached by an admirer who'd rather be looking up at you than at what's happening on the stage.

Whether you hit it off with a music lover, a professional musician or someone who plays for pleasure at the local bar or café, music is the link for potentially a very good love connection for you. At an intimate gig, sit close enough to make eye contact with the performer. If he's cute you could invite him for a drink at the interval as a thank you for the music, and you might be making beautiful music together before too long.

Make sure to include concert halls in your location checklist and festivals too, where you have the double whammy of being outdoors as well, to your list of locations to find a partner. Gone are the days of slumming it at festivals. You can go 'glamping' (glamorous camping) in smart, well-equipped tents or stay in a hotel or B&B off site and travel in. So don't rule out a summer of love, sunshine and outdoorsy music, especially if it's not something you've tried before.

You could take the music theme one step further and join a band or a singing group. Singing is a great release of tension too so it's a good personal exercise to help you loosen up a bit. And the guy with the gorgeous deep voice that makes your toes tingle could end up duetting with you for life, if you're lucky and time things right. Remember to check out your best times for love, to orchestrate your get-togethers.

One-on-one singing lessons or learning to play an instrument may also open up your romantic opportunities.

4. Get Banking

There's no getting away from it. Let's talk money. It is particularly important to your sign, and as it helps you feel stable and secure more than most other signs it seems natural that someone who deals with finances should play a major part in your romantic life.

If you haven't got a cent to your name because something in your personal astrological chart makes you spend your cash as soon as you've earned it, there's no reason why a sympathetic financial counselor couldn't be the man for you.

It's more likely though that you'll find love in line at the bank. Sometimes it can feel like you're waiting forever to be served, giving you ample time to get into conversation with someone you like the look of waiting in line with you, or even the bank teller at the counter. And someone who deals with bonds, stocks and shares could totally be the man for you.

This isn't about greed at all or snapping up a man for what he owns or earns rather than for his kindness, personality and loving ways. It's just about having some security for the future as you like to plan ahead and, luckily, the right man for you does too.

And if you believe that what goes around comes around, it may pay you to be generous when it comes to charities. Even collectors on the street trying to raise cash donations or asking you to sign up for some worthwhile cause are worth a moment of your time, a little of your money and perhaps a piece of your heart too.

Getting involved with causes that deal with national heritage, including the kind that helps to fund the restoration of grand but faded buildings, is another way to open up your dating options. Your sign is usually financially canny and hard working too, so you'd be an asset to this kind of organization and may find yourself in the company of your ideal man as a result.

5. Get into Food

Unless you're one of those Capricorns whose personal chart makes you a real foodie (check out where your Venus sign is) it's quite possible that you sometimes forget to eat because you're so driven by work, or that your larder has just the bare necessities because a) it's only fuel or b) there's no point cooking just for one so why bother?

Think again, as changing your grocery shopping habits can change your love life and, believe it or not, you could meet the man of your dreams while you're shopping for food.

You seek quality in your partner so head to the smarter super-markets where there's more variety and richer pickings on the food front as well as on the man front. Or investigate long estab-lished, family-run shops that may hold more interest for you and for the kind of man you seek, as you both value enterprises that offer personal service and are almost dynasty-like, handed on from generation to generation.

And as good value is something you look for everywhere in life, consider natural and organic options at a farmers market. This also gives you another chance to connect with an earthy, outdoorsy farmer or market gardener who could be just right for you.

Or you could meet him on a wine tasting course so you know what to order in restaurants or what to serve when your hot date comes around for dinner, as the object of this exercise is for you to mingle with delicious potential soulmates and to taste delicacies that you've possibly never tried before.

If you like to eat out, romance may blossom with anyone from a fellow diner, to the restaurant owner, to the person taking your order or with the chef cooking your meal. So praise good service and become a regular customer if love looks like it could be on the menu.

Even your local candy store has the potential for you to bump into the love of your life because, strange as it may sound, your future sweetheart is likely to have a sweet tooth.

6. Get Moving

Moving in this case means moving house. It's a big ask but think about your current situation. Are you still living with parents? Being at home with your folks is likely to cramp your love style.

And if you're renting with friends, it can be awkward trying to juggle schedules, bathroom rotas and that tricky moment in the morning when you both emerge from the bedroom.

Maybe it's time to splash out and get a place of your own and some privacy,

If you're single and living where you never get to meet anyone because you're working long hours and commuting, try to get a place nearer to where you work and to some sociable things to do, perhaps a friendly local coffee bar with music nights which ties into your 'Get Musical' option too.

The same goes for you if you're divorced or separated and still living in the former family home. You could be bogged down by stagnant energy if you've found it hard to move on emotionally from an ex, so get all the clutter connected to that relationship out of the way to allow space for something new and someone better to come into your life.

Better yet, a new home means a completely fresh start. You may even find you click with the guy helping you to buy or sell your place. One newly divorced Capricorn client of mine put her home on the market and ended up marrying the rather lovely man who sold her house for her, so it can happen.

Once you've found your new place, or even if you do have to stay put, decorate it to let your personality and sensuality shine through.

Make your bedroom in particular a boudoir built for love. Make it grown up and gorgeous as at some point you'll be inviting Mr. Right in, and a line-up of plush toys on the bed is definitely not good feng shui when it comes to romance. Redecorating also connects you to the antiques, home design and decor options mentioned so this is definitely an 'on message' way to bring love into your life.

If you're doing up an old place that needs some tender loving care, make sure you get contractors in who feel the same way, as if you don't gel with them the energy they put into your home may have a negative effect and you'll always be thinking of the grief they gave you over the bathroom taps rather than enjoying a long relaxing soak in the tub after a long day. And if you do get on with the guys working on your property they're much more likely to do a better job for you, and it could even lead to building a romance with your builder, or sowing the seeds of love with your garden designer.

Having solid foundations in life is a big thing for your sign, literally, so getting together romantically with your architect if it's a new-build or a fixer-upper that needs major restoration (which is more likely as you resonate better with old properties) could make this an earth-moving romantic experience for you in every way.

7. Get Green

There's a good chance that you could meet the love of your life wherever green or ecological issues are involved.

Yours is one of the signs that completely appreciates that the world's resources are limited, so not wasting them or abusing them is a pretty good idea.

You're likely to buy quality clothes that are timeless classics so they last, and you'll squeeze your toothpaste tube until it's unrecognizable in your efforts to get every last drop and value for money before you finally dispose of it.

So anywhere that recycles things is a good place for you to meet a potential partner. Vintage fashion shops are ideal haunts, especially if they run entertainments events like nostalgia evenings where you get to wear retro clothes and eat the food and dance to the music of a bygone age.

Places or people who deal in classic cars also hold romantic possibilities for you.

And rather than throw away favorite shoes and household gadgets or jewelry, wherever you can get them repaired could be where you meet your love match. Either the repairer or another customer who shares your 'save the planet' mindset could be made for you.

Even investing in a composter for your garden waste is another option that could, strangely enough, put you in touch with guys who are on your romantic wavelength.

Or you might meet Mr. Right while you're trying to save a classic if crumbling old building from being demolished to make way for an apartment block. You'd be fantastic as a negotiator in a green campaign as your poker face would give nothing way, although this is also something you may need to be aware of in loving relationships too.

Don't be afraid to show your passion and your feelings as being distant or too controlling may be what's sent misleading signals to would-be partners in the past. Even in a campaign situation, sometimes an ounce of emotion is worth more than a raft of reasoned and logical debate.

The bottom line then is to make your space a greener place. If you do, you're putting yourself on the right path to find true love.

Location Checklist

A checklist is a handy way to get you focused and pinpoint those places you might add to your schedule in order to help love along. This is not an exhaustive list by any means but will give you some ideas, and help you think of many more along similar lines. You could meet 'the one' at a:

- Food fair
- Organic market
- Reclamation center
- DIY store
- Opera
- Jazz gig
- Music festival
- Country walk
- Flower show
- Garden center
- Deli
- Smart restaurant
- Antiques store
- Art class
- Art gallery
- Wine tasting
- Charity fund-raising event

- Environmental campaign

When you've found your perfect partner, look back on this and smile at the memory of the time you hooked up with that guy who was putting up posters in your favorite coffee house about a charity auction. He took you to dinner at the oldest family-run restaurant in town, and before long you ended up buying a run down but romantic old house to renovate and live in together, forever. And the rest is history. Insert your own romantic 'how we met' story instead, of course.

Chapter 11

Where to Find Love if You're Aquarius

You're one of the free spirits of the zodiac. You have your own style, your own outlook on life and, truth be told, you don't really like to be tied down even though you are looking for a loving connection with someone special.

Sometimes your spontaneity and 'living for the moment' mindset get the better of you and you rush into things with your heart full of hope and your head full of optimism, only for things to fall apart when you realize that someone isn't what you thought they were. Or they try to change you or push you into a more traditional role than you imagined for yourself, which makes you feel claustrophobic.

So the key thing for you in order to take romance further is to spend a little more time to get to know someone as a friend first. You are fantastic as a friend, one of the best signs to have as a best friend precisely because you take people at face value until, or unless, they mess up.

Until now you may have been drawn to men who expected you always to be there for them and make them the center of your universe. Your easygoing nature may have allowed you to go along with that at first, but you're not the type to live in anyone's shadow and soon the need to break out and do your own thing, your own way, may have taken over leaving your bewildered lover wondering what just happened.

While you love being with someone who can be entertaining and who adds variety to your life, any hint of neediness is a real turn-off for you. Yes, you want to be needed, but not in a suffo-cating way and certainly not in a way that tries to make you fit into some kind of box. In fact, 'ticking boxes' and 'thinking outside the box' are quite possibly among your least favorite phrases. For you, there simply is no box and you can't and won't be pigeonholed or categorized.

A partner who makes you think, who shares ideas, who surprises you in good ways at every turn and who understands that although you need some freedom at times, you'll always come back to him, is just what you need.

To find a man who's more on your wavelength, you may not have to go too far, but there may be some more lessons for you to learn about love along the way. Try the following options to put you in the right place to meet the right sort of partner who can deal with your idiosyncrasies and still be completely in love with you because of them, not despite them.

Start looking now, because he's closer than you think.

1. Get Local

Other signs may do better in the love stakes if they take a trip abroad or broaden their horizons to meet a man from another country or culture. You, however, are in the fortunate position of being almost able to walk out of your front door and bump into the man who could be your partner for life.

He could be a neighbor or a friend of one of your siblings, if you have them, or either of these two could help to play cupid and set you up with your dream date who might, in fact, be one of a pair of twins.

Your best bet is to try to shop and socialize locally rather than look further afield to find love, as your ideal guy is likely to be in a neighborhood coffee bar with his laptop, in a bar holding forth on some fascinating piece of news of the day, or browsing through the magazines and newspapers section in the local bookstore.

He's the kind of man who loves to be kept informed and mentally stimulated, which is where you come in with your quirky ideas, love of anything new and sometimes outrageous or at least unexpected ways. This includes random public displays of affection rather than more scandalous behavior, though anything could be possible as you'll be a potent combination once you're together.

You could find him by getting involved in community projects, especially any that meet at local schools, or at an arts center poetry night, comedy night or literary event.

None of these things might be your thing, but your own unique selling point is that you're usually game for anything new, and you'll give even the most peculiar event a try just because it is different. In fact the weirder-sounding the occasion, the better it may be for you to go to it.

Don't believe it? A top TV comedian (the type of man who would be ideal for you) started his career with a touring show which was so off-the-wall it attracted only a handful of people to see it, so he invited the whole audience out afterwards for a drink on the proceeds to thank them for turning up. An Aquarius friend of mine was in that tiny audience and hit it off with him, and they started dating.

This is exactly the sort of random, unexpected thing that could happen to you, so keep an open mind. Think quirky and local, and be on the lookout for a chatty, witty guy as he could be just the one you've been waiting for.

2. Get Mobile

While your chances of finding love are good if you stay local, it's inevitable that you're going to be on the move at some point.

If you're driving, you might spot the man of your dreams as you're waiting in a traffic jam. Or you could find your heart beats faster because of the vehicle rescue service guy who's helped you out with your broken-down car. Alternatively, it could be someone you meet at the auto shop it's towed to so you can have your car repaired.

The underlying philosophy here is firstly to look for the silver lining behind the cloud, but also that your sign in particular could meet your ideal man in unexpected circumstances connected to travel.

Get talking to people on buses and don't read on a long train journey, instead get into conversation with the cute guy sitting next to you. But do get your book or magazine out as a talking point because he's likely to be well-read so you have an instant conversation starter, as you're the type to be reading something unusual and he's the type to notice.

Short hops and local travel are your best bet. You could even find love at a taxi stand where a simple comment about the weather could see you sharing a cab and maybe, before too long, sharing your lives together.

Romance is under your nose, you just have to be alert to it. Mr. Right could be a fellow passenger on your regular commute. He could be a train driver, a ticket inspector, a cab driver or airline pilot traveling to the airport by train.

Cycling is another great way for you to connect with your future partner. If you want to get fit, join a cycling club where you're bound to meet equally fit cycling fans, and you'll get to see some amazing local countryside on weekend rides too.

If cycling doesn't appeal, then the simplest way of getting about of all is walking or, ideally, rambling or hiking. The man for you tends to move fast though so a running club might be an even better place for you to meet your match.

And if that sounds too much like hard work, you might find love with a petrol-head. You'll encounter him wherever classic cars race or at Formula One tracks. It's not unlikely that, with your sign's eclectic tastes, you own an unusual car so getting together with your VW Beetle Owner's Club might also get your love-life back on the road.

3. Get Learning

One of the best places for you to meet someone special is wherever you can learn something new. You might hit it off with the tutor or a fellow student, or you might be the one doing the teaching in an adult education class. Whichever it is, love could be on the curriculum.

A language course is particularly well-starred for you, as classes where you just get your head down and study are not as helpful to finding the right kind of relationship for you as ones where there's interaction and discussion. Brushing up on Shakespeare could be just the thing, especially if you get to read the lines for Juliet to some gorgeous guy's Romeo.

You might want to return to study in order to get a promotion or change career. Or if you're not as computer savvy as you think you should be, pick a course to get you up to speed. And if you're already a techno genius there's always some new software you could benefit from finding out how to use. This could apply to your job too so look out for eligible IT training guys at work.

Or you might want to study a design program to make your own website. It's an ideal way to meet like-minded people, both by learning how to construct a site as well as by connecting to others who want to see what you have to say, sell, do or promote on the web.

It might pay you to get in touch with old school friends on the internet too. However you felt about school when you were there, it's possible that meeting up with former classmates online or at a school reunion could pave the way to romance for you.

And since you like the extreme and the unexpected, you could take up an unusual study like astrology or graphology. Your sign's ruling planet Uranus also rules the art of astrology so it's something you have a natural affinity for, and the skill of reading handwriting would appeal to your quirky nature and would also be a great party trick.

You could meet Mr. Right on a course to learn these skills, and both options have a practical benefit in that they'd also give you an insight into the man of your dreams once you've found him. Even guys who say they're not interested in the stars love to be told about their own sign so astrology can be a great conversation starter, and graphology gives you a perfect reason to get him to write down his name and number.

4. Get Communicating

Words mean a lot to the man you're destined to hook up with. The chances are he loves to talk, but even if he turns out to be a man of few words you can be sure they'll be worth waiting to hear.

You could meet him on an internet dating site, where your usual unusual approach could cause quite a stir. Emails and SMS messages are the way to your ideal man's heart so a romance that starts via this route has a good chance of going on to the next level.

Regular mail has good connections for you too so if you have deliveries made to your home, check out the delivery guy or the postman especially if there's a chance he'll be knocking on your door on a regular basis, as things could develop into something more. Or you could meet Mr. Right while you're waiting in line at the post office.

Online fantasy gaming, especially sci-fi role-playing, may also hold romantic potential.

And your local newspaper office is another prime location for romance. If you need to place a small ad then phone or place it in person rather than online. You might meet one of their journalists on his way to a story and end up with a photo of you together in the wedding pages before long.

Look out for men in the media in general, whether he's an advertising or print rep, an author or a presenter. Your nearest bookstore, already mentioned in 'Get Local', is another place to hang out either to meet him if he's a writer at a book-signing or someone who may be a fan of your favorite author's work.

Just look for connections. Some will be obvious, others are much more subtle but if you think about them after you've found your Significant Other, you can be sure that the stars will have put you where you needed to be to meet him.

5. Get Motivated

You're a great person for getting people together. It's one of your sign's unique selling points. Even though you can, at times, feel aloof and too unusual yourself to really be part of the crowd, you're more charismatic and have more influence than you may realize.

So if there's an issue you feel strongly about, particularly if it's a local one, perhaps a school being closed down, library services being cut, local businesses threatened, or animals in distress, then get involved in organizing a group to challenge, highlight and put right whatever the situation is.

Joining forces with others is a great way to stand as a united front and, potentially, to bond with someone special. It's a fact that people connect more quickly and deeply (and romantically) in adversity. The survival instinct kicks in, which can be frustratingly slower to happen when things are going well.

Get together especially to produce leaflets, flyers and posters that you can hand deliver or put up in shop windows. Circulating like this is a good way to expand your network of acquaintances and friends and that's a big part of expanding and changing your love style experiences.

If you've never considered taking a stand like this, it can be a real eye-opener. You may find yourself writing to newspapers, being involved in protests or challenging people's opinions at local meetings. All the while you're doing this, you're making new connections.

And it doesn't have to be dull. In the UK, groups got together in town centers and, dressed as badgers, they danced the *Harlem Shake* to draw attention to proposed plans to cull the badger population. A flash mob event like this could be entirely your thing as it's quirky, unexpected, entertaining and newsworthy, plus there's the possibility of romance.

Or you could be the one responsible for arranging campaign meetings, as well as having regular social gatherings where you leave the main agenda at the door and just have fun.

You most likely already live in the same area as him and you're definitely on the same wavelength, so the chances of finding a guy who has even more in common with you are high. All you need to do is find your cause and get involved.

6. Get Doubled Up

Though you cherish your independence, finding a soulmate can be much more enjoyable and more successful when you do it with friends, especially in your case as your sign has a knack for acquiring lots of acquaintances.

Some you'll just go to the movies with, others you'll open your heart to about your man troubles, and still more will be happy to be your wing woman when you're on the lookout for a guy. That may sound predatory, but you can be certain there's someone out there with his wing man looking for you. So hunt in pairs. You may find you hit it off with twins or at least with two best friends, so double dating (or a double wedding) could be twice the fun.

The same goes for speed-dating evenings, which could also work for you as you're spontaneous and make quick decisions, and the man of your dreams is a fast talker so you'll both know within minutes if you're suited to one another. Your sign is often quite happy to go to events solo, but it's good to have a friend along on a speed-dating evening, whether you hit it off with someone or not.

Make a point of meeting your friends' friends too as it could surprise you who they've not introduced you to, thinking you'd have nothing in common. Just having that friend linking you both is enough to feel comfortable about the connection in your case.

Also think about doing things just for two. Hire a tandem bicycle with a guy friend that you'd like to get to know better, or strap yourself to a skydiving friend of a friend for a doubled-up jump out of an airplane. Do it for charity to give you an added incentive, not that being hooked up to a handsome skydiver isn't already a good enough reason.

And do a double-take and look again at your own guy friends because there's every possibility that one of them could be the man for you, you just haven't realized it yet.

Friendship is extremely important to you and it's unlikely that you'll find lasting true love without a solid friendship first, despite your spontaneous ways. So if he's a pal already it's an even easier leap to become a soulmate as half the work's already done.

7. Get Playing

You should know by now that words are a source of pleasure to the man you're trying to attract and there's a strong chance that the same goes for you. You might be great at crosswords or, more likely, a collector of trivia and bizarre facts that come in handy when you least expect it.

Trivia becomes useful knowledge and information if you put it to use on a bar or coffee shop quiz team and you can astound guys with your endless stream of odd but engaging facts and figures. You might know the names of all the horses that have won a particular major race since it began. An Aquarian friend of mine regularly dazzles male admirers with such information. But simply knowing your TV soap story lines and movie stars could make you the perfect addition to a team of guys who only know about sport.

Or have a games evening at home where you get to show off your talents. Add your own unique twist to standard games with speed checkers or blindfolded Jenga. Dress up as Miss Scarlet or Colonel Mustard if you're playing Clue. And if you've never played Twister now's your chance.

Try electronic games too, like Wii, guaranteed to bring out the competitive techno geek if not in you then certainly in your guy pals who'll want to play at the toughest level.

And if you can arrange your games night to coincide with your best love times then romance becomes less of a game of chance, more of a sure thing.

Location Checklist

A checklist is a handy way to focus your direction and pinpoint those places you need to add to your routine in order to help love along. This is not an exhaustive list but will give you some ideas, and help you think of many more along similar lines. You could meet 'the one' at a:

- Graphology course
- Tandem cycle ride
- Speed dating
- Motorbike riding
- Car repair center
- Astrology class
- Skydiving
- Science fiction bookstore
- Home delivery service
- Local newspaper
- IT course
- Flash mob event
- Language course
- School reunion
- Taxi stand

When you've found your perfect partner, look back on this and smile at the memory of the time you met your man on the graphology course. You could tell by the way he looped his letters he was a very sexy guy. On your first date he picked you up on his motorbike and took you skydiving, wrapping you in his arms in the air until you made the perfect landing. And the rest is history. Insert your own romantic 'how we met' story instead, of course.

Chapter 12

Where to Find Love if You're Pisces

If there were anyone more ready, willing and able to give love than you, they'd be hard to find. Your sign can be the most selfless in love, better at giving rather than taking. You're deeply romantic and sensitive and would truly give your all to make your loved one happy.

Your watery sign is dreamy, floaty and intuitive, and works best when you're allowed to go with the flow. So rather than make waves you often prefer to take the more passive line in a relationship which can mean that what you want tends to get neglected.

You easily pick up on other people's moods and feelings so will all too readily adapt yourself to accommodate them in order to keep the peace. Sometimes you may feel like you no longer even recognize yourself or know what you want because, chameleon-like, you've had to change or adapt so often to keep other people happy. Which, with your sign, may be where the problem of finding lasting love lies.

Giving up your own needs to satisfy your other half's needs, wants and desires is a beautiful thing but one that, after time, can lead to resentment.

It's also quite likely that in the past you've been drawn to men who were very precise and perhaps rather critical of you, how you look or how you go about doing things. And it's easy to get into a repeating cycle where that's the kind of treatment you expect.

That's where this book is going to help you out and put you in the arms of someone who cares and feels things as deeply as you do, instinctively rather than analytically.

The right partner for you understands and encourages you to

be self-nurturing, positive and optimistic, rather than believing you have to give way every time.

To be fair, there is a little bit of the martyr about you and if you're completely honest with yourself it's a role you sometimes like to play. It gives you an odd sense of power, as in, "Well I've given this up for you so now you owe me". Not that you ever really expect payback.

People tend to lean on you, especially in times of distress, and whether you know it or not you have a real ability to soothe and heal. There's nothing wrong with loving men who are in need, and often it can't be helped because they're drawn to your calming, all-encompassing energy like a thirsty man to a well.

But think about whether it's doing you any good and consider breaking those patterns and finding new places to meet a new kind of man.

This time you're going to get it right. Set your boundaries and don't allow the wrong type to cross them, as you may have done in the past.

Trust your highly intuitive instincts, check when the stars are aligning in your favor for love and you won't be disappointed. That loving, caring, sharing man you've been waiting for has been treading water too, but not because he needs rescuing from life's stormy seas. He just wants you to dive right in and enjoy life together with him.

1. Get Cozy At Home

One of the best places for you to meet your match is at your home. It could be with the guy who comes to install a shower, fix the plumbing or, if you're lucky, to put in a swimming pool.

Home food deliveries are also a potential source of romance, whether it's the man who drops off the grocery shopping you've ordered online or the cute guy who delivers your pizza.

It's an idea to make a point of inviting people over for a meal, though a small gathering would fit the bill better for you than a lavish affair. You won't have so much competition from others and can give potential admirers your full attention. If you wanted to tip the scales in your favor make sure you add some aphrodisiac items to the menu. Oysters, strawberries and champagne should help move things along nicely.

Your mother might want to play matchmaker, so why not let her try? It's quite possible that she knows you better than you know yourself, and she'd certainly want to see you with someone fabulous as he'll be part of her family too.

You could also find the love of your life in a DIY store, as he may be someone who renovates houses or owns properties that he develops or rents out. Kitchen and bathroom departments are where he's most likely to be found.

If you rent or own a holiday home near the sea, this could also be where you meet your match. It doesn't even have to be your own home. Just remember that water and where you live, even if it's only temporarily, are the key factors to finding love.

So if you spot a damp patch on the ceiling or the tub overflows, don't despair. It could be the very thing to bring your knight in shining armor to your door and into your life. And as he turns up to repair the damage to your ceiling, he could also be helping to mend your bruised and battered heart.

The house-selling industry also has a lot of potential for you in the romance department. You might have a powerful connection with someone who comes to buy your home, or decide to change career, work as a real estate agent and fall in love with a client.

Also be on the lookout for men who live in unusual places or whose homes are like a protective shell, so someone who lives in a castle would be ideal! A guy who lives near water and is a great cook could truly be the one for you, and he's a real catch if his home is a houseboat or he has a home complete with sea view.

2. Get into Water

As a water sign, anything, anyone and anywhere connected to H_2O is potentially a clue that love is nearby for you.

Pack a picnic for a day out on the beach or by a river, and bring extra to share as you may well hook up with someone who enjoys your food as much as your company. Add your swimsuit too as you really are in your element in water, with the power of a mythical mermaid to attract your lover with your siren call.

Make regular trips to your local pool and join a swimming club as these would both be great for your health as well as your love life. If you're a good swimmer you could perhaps consider teaching adults or their children life-saving skills as single dads would be glad to have you on board with their family. And if you can't swim this is a perfect time to learn and add to your talents.

Or you could take up sailing or rowing as these will get you mixing with some fit and active guys too. And walking along coastal paths could help you spot seals, whales or dolphins as well as a potential soulmate.

You could try fishing, and land yourself a fisherman or the skipper of the fishing boat. Even fishmongers can't be ruled out in the love stakes.

If travel is more your thing, choose a cruise and get cozy with the captain. It doesn't have to be a luxury trip as you could just as easily find love on an adventure vacation, gliding along on a basic felucca down the Nile in Egypt, or in a rowboat in the park.

You can even send out the watery vibes by wearing jewelry made from shells or pearls and wearing sea-green colors, eau de nil shades and ocean blues to give yourself the aura of a sea goddess. It's another way to bring a man who loves the sea into your life, believe it or not. You intuitive watery types can sense each other miles away but a few subtle signals can help seal the deal.

3. Get Cooking

If you're a typical Pisces you love to share and there's no better way to share than with food. It's sociable, it's sensual (or can be in the right situation), and it's a physical necessity, so what's not to like?

For some Pisces, cooking can be a chore but not if you see it as a way to your future man's heart. This whole experience of finding love is also about extending yourself, getting you out of a romantic rut and pushing you towards new ideas and adding new skills to your repertoire. So whether you care for cooking or don't know a spatula from a saucepan, book yourself onto a cooking course, ideally one specializing in seafood.

Some seafoods are seen as love enhancers, especially oysters, lobsters and conch, and as it tends to be men who want to learn more about the more intricate arts of cooking you'd be in some excellent male company as you learn from scratch or, if you're already accomplished in the kitchen, enhance your talents.

You might also have the added pleasure of going to the docks to select fresh fish for your menu, so ideally choose a culinary venue that's close to the sea, which gives you a double whammy of sea and seafood, both of which are conducive to finding your ideal mate.

If you're vegetarian, or are allergic to fish, try a cookery course that suits you, still by the sea if possible. Making comfort food, cakes and cookies, food like Mom used to make, can still be the way to a guy's heart, or learning to cook up healthier options could connect you with a more sensitive, soulful type.

Restaurants beside water are a great option for you too, especially for an organized dating dinner night. It's like speed dating but with food. If you're single, you might be perfectly happy having lunch or coffee on your own somewhere nice but going out for dinner at a restaurant full of couples, groups and happy families can sometimes feel awkward. Look online or in your local press to find restaurants offering this service and get booked in. Better still, see if you can tie in the experience to fall on one of your best love days.

4. Get in Touch with Your Heritage

If you want to find the man for you, look to the past. The right guy for you has a passion for ancient sites, castles, historic buildings, romantic ruined towers and history.

He might be an historian, someone who renovates old, unloved properties, or is a master craftsman employed by preservation societies to put treasured buildings back into their original shape and condition.

Chances are you too have a respect for the past as your sign understands karmically that where we came from is relevant to who we are, or who we'd like to become. Even if you don't quite get that theory, you're very sensitive to the resonances of old buildings, and can sometimes feel like you're in touch with the past just by walking through them. It's as if you soak up the energy from previous generations that has gone into making the property what it is today. You may even be sensitive enough to feel whether a place is haunted.

So how does this put you in touch with the man of your dreams? If he's not renovating the place, he could be a tour guide, or he could be the owner of a home whose family has lived there for generations.

He could be the chef or a fellow diner at the on-site café or he could be someone persuading you to contribute to fund-raising money for preserving similar properties.

Another way to look at this is to start researching your family tree. Although you can do this solo online it would be better to work with others who have expertise in this area as that's how you're more likely to make connections, romantic or otherwise. It's a fascinating way to find out about yourself and your background, and discovering more about your roots can help you analyze your own relationships and how they work. You could even find you learn from the mistakes of your family's past so you don't make the same mistakes when you meet your own Mr. Right.

5. Get Healing

It's embedded in your nature to care for others, as you often seem to pick up on people's hurts and unspoken troubles and can lend a sympathetic ear or a shoulder to cry on.

This is a wonderful personality trait, and makes you a great carer, counselor and healer. You probably give out this vibe all day every day without noticing it as it's second nature to you. Strangers may tell you their troubles at the bus stop or in the doctor's surgery (sometimes with way too much information!) but you can handle it.

There are a number of ways you can use this ability to put yourself in the right place at the right time to find the right man. He might just be that person in line or at a café who feels he can talk to you, and your gentle, understanding ways may make him see you in a loving light. You do tend to attract lost souls who want to be taken care of so do be careful not to take on men who drain your energy and give little back.

Becoming a volunteer or working in a caring environment could help you meet a potential soulmate who would appreciate your soothing manner. Friends or relatives of those in your care might put you on a pedestal for your kindness and dedication, or guys you work with in a caring or nurturing capacity could see you in a romantic light.

This may not sound particularly glamorous, and a lot of it must come from the heart, but often that's the way love happens. While you're giving selflessly to someone in need, you're magnetically drawing in someone else somewhere who wants to do the same for you.

It also may sound like there's a lot of giving but not a lot of being given to going on. Because you pick up on other people's moods so easily, it can be quite energy-sapping for you so consider spending some time in a quiet place to recharge your batteries, ideally somewhere you can be with others but still have peace and tranquility.

You could stay in a sanctuary, try a silent retreat, or spend time in an ancient monastery or spiritual location abroad, perhaps in India. You'll feel rejuvenated and you're likely to meet people, including guys, who are on your wavelength. You're likely to rub shoulders (literally, if you learn a soothing massage skill there too) with new friends from all over the world, who feel at home in a caring, creative and nurturing environment. And you'll be so relaxed and recharged that you'll be sending out all the right signals to potential partners.

And if that's all too much, treat yourself to a reflexology session or consider learning how to do it for others. The feet are ruled by Pisces so, odd as it may sound, the way to your soulmate could be through the sole.

6. Get Creative

You're incredibly creative, whether you're aware of that or not, so investigating this part of your personality could take you in a new direction, straight to the heart of Mr. Right.

Photography and watercolor painting in particular are great ways for you to express yourself. Both options attract creative, imaginative men, should you wish to learn these skills alongside them on a course.

It could pay you to specialize in beach scenes, moody black and white images of long stretches of empty sand and amazing dark skies, laden with emotion rather than conventionally pretty pictures. You're a very deep person and bringing out that depth in a visual way is not only therapeutic for you but may also send a signal to the right kind of man that there's an almost spiritual connection with him through your artistic vision of the world.

Exhibiting your work could become a money-making hobby if

you put your mind to it. You could consider selling indiv
framed images to small, boutique-style homewares stores
kind of man who would suit you likes to have special things in
his home. We're thinking big here but anything is possible. It's
also a way of raising your confidence and self-esteem, which
adds to your attraction.

A regular stall at a craft or design could help you meet your
match. That gorgeous man picking out shell bracelets and
necklaces from your range could be buying for his daughter or
sister so he's free for you and he clearly has good taste! You could
even encounter him on the beach as you collect shells and
driftwood to create your pieces.

Creating art is like putting your soul on show, in the raw, and
it's beautiful. So if the idea of selling it seems like selling out, do
it for the sheer pleasure of expressing yourself. You could also tie
this in with art as therapy, making it a double whammy in the
search for romance as it connects to the healing side of your
nature as well.

And remember that dance is an expression of creativity and
love too, and a great way to merge with someone who feels the
rhythm of life the way you do.

7. Get In Touch With The Moon

Night time and the moon are extremely powerful for you in your
quest for love. Water signs like your own are particularly
sensitive to the phases of the moon and it could pay you, more
than most, to keep an eye on what's happening in the stars so you
can be in tune with them down on planet Earth. 'As above, so
below' is a favorite and powerful astrology mantra.

You're also often at your best at night, as your senses are
heightened in the dark and your sign especially is tuned into
dreams, magic, mystery and illusion, the stuff that night time
and moonlight are made of.

Look for or organize events that get you out in the moonlight with others. Try a moonlit horse ride or full moon kayaking.

If you're traveling, try places like Thailand or Ibiza where full moon parties are a big thing. There's a tendency for these parties to get a little crazy with wild dancing, but dancing is great for your sign, so don't rule this out as a place to meet your soulmate. Do keep your wits about you, because in nature animals behave unusually boldly under the influence of the full moon and it can lead to uncharacteristic behavior in humans too.

Moonlit fishing may also be an option, as the moon and the water are a perfect combination for you when it comes to romance. You could take that a step further and go for a moonlight swim with others, skinny-dipping if you're daring enough with wild swimming clubs who get together to swim in beautiful, unspoilt parts of the world. Check online to see if there's one near you, as this could be a way to meet your ideal man.

Moonlight always makings things more romantic. If you get the chance to visit Venice in Italy, take a moonlit gondola ride. It's a dreamy way to explore this city of water. If your timing is right and it falls during one of your best love phases that's when you could find your Mr. Right too.

Once you have found the right man and if he's dragging his heels over taking things further, the full moon may well prompt a moment of madness and a marriage proposal. And if you want to start something new, with someone new, do it on a new moon as this has the best astrological energy for new beginnings. It can also help to harness the power of a new moon by making a wish-list of things you'd like in your life, and in love. Check your diary for the monthly new and full moon dates or visit www.orlilysen.com for more information.

If you're really into gardening, you might want to learn about planting by the moon phases. This isn't as crazy as it sounds. Certain beauty products companies, including Dr Hauschka Skin Care, harvest their ingredients biodynamically, by the phases of the moon. So instead of an Ibiza-style full moon rave, you could organize a more serene full moon vegetable patch party to meet the man of your dreams.

You might also find him camping by a river or beach, if you're the outdoorsy type. He'll be the guy cooking up some fabulous food on a simple camping stove by the light of the full moon, and he could be the very man you've been looking for.

Location Checklist

A checklist is a handy way to focus your direction and pinpoint those places you need to add to your routine in order to help love along. This is not an exhaustive list but will give you some ideas, and help you think of many more along similar lines. You could find 'the one' at a:

- Moonlit horse ride
- Camping by a river
- Heritage home
- Your home
- By the sea
- Homewares store
- Family-run business
- Full moon party
- Dinner party at a friend's home
- Cookery course
- Fishmongers
- Swimming pool
- Ocean cruise
- Sanctuary
- Photography course
- Researching your family tree
- Charitable trust
- Watercolor painting course

When you've found your perfect partner, look back on this and smile at the memory of the time you met him buying fish, fresh off the boats at the dock, where you were taking photos. He invited you to try his home-cooking and you shared dinner under the stars at his place, ending the first of many dates with a magical moonlit kiss. And the rest is history. Insert your own romantic 'how we met' story instead, of course.

Chapter 13

Find Your Venus Sign and Your Supercharged Venus Love Years

Wherever the planet Venus falls in your personal horoscope chart shows what and who you love. It's easy to find out which sign Venus is in for you from the list below. First look for the year you were born, then the date that covers that sign. So if you were born on 7 June 1962 your Venus sign is Cancer. All times are in GMT, so if you were born outside the UK you need to convert this to the corresponding local time where you were born to accurately pinpoint your Venus sign. You can do this online back to 1970 at www.timeanddate.com or if you get stuck you can contact www.orlilysen.com.

Which House is Your Venus Sign In?

Knowing which sign Venus is in for you will give you ample insight into your love style, but if you want to know even more you can find out which house it's in too.

A horoscope chart is divided into twelve houses, each of which represents a different area of life. Think of it as like a pizza divided into twelve slices, each with a different topping and flavor.

Depending on when and where you were born, Venus will be in one of these houses (or slices), and whichever one that is tells you more about your love style and preferences.

You can only really see how this works in a personal chart so you'll need to go online and search for 'generate your own free astrological birth chart'. Key in your name, where you were born and your date and time of birth. The more accurate your birth time, the more accurate your chart will be.

Starting from the middle of the left hand side of the chart

where there should be a thicker, darker dividing line, count downwards and anticlockwise (from left to right) to find out which house, from one to twelve, your Venus sign is in. Some charts have the houses already numbered, which makes it easier. The symbol for Venus is a circle on top of a cross. Once you've identified your Venus sign from the list of dates below, for example if it's in Gemini and your chart shows it's in the 8th house, read the chapter on 'Who to love if you have Venus in Gemini' and look at the 8th house section for more information about the man you're most compatible with.

Don't worry if for any reason you can't access your chart. This isn't essential in your quest for romance, but it can give you a little more insight into the right kind of man for you.

When is Your Venus Cycle Strongest?

Your love life improves and finding someone to love is a whole lot easier if the love planet is already working in your favor. Venus is at her strongest for you every seven years so when your age is a multiple of seven then your love luck is in. So that's if you're: 7, 14, 21, 28, 35, 42, 49, 56, 63, 70, 77, 84, 91, 98. Make a note of when you're in a strong Venus cycle and add it to the checklist at the back of the book.

Find Your Venus Sign

1940

Jan 18 14:00	Pisces
Feb 12 05:51	Aries
Mar 08 16:25	Taurus
Apr 04 18:10	Gemini
May 06 18:47	Cancer
Jul 05 16:17	Gemini
Aug 01 02:20	Cancer
Sep 08 16:59	Leo

Oct 06 21:10   Virgo
Nov 01 17:24   Libra
Nov 26 12:32   Scorpio
Dec 20 19:36   Sagittarius

1941

Jan 13 21:29   Capricorn
Feb 06 21:49   Aquarius
Mar 02 22:33   Pisces
Mar 27 00:58   Aries
Apr 20 05:53   Taurus
May 14 13:36   Gemini
Jun 07 23:53   Cancer
Jul 02 12:33   Leo
Jul 27 04:12   Virgo
Aug 21 00:29   Libra
Sep 15 04:01   Scorpio
Oct 10 19:21   Sagittarius
Nov 06 10:17   Capricorn
Dec 05 23:04   Aquarius

1942

Apr 06 13:14   Pisces
May 06 02:26   Aries
Jun 02 00:26   Taurus
Jun 27 22:18   Gemini
Jul 23 06:10   Cancer
Aug 17 03:04   Leo
Sep 10 14:38   Virgo
Oct 04 18:58   Libra
Oct 28 18:40   Scorpio
Nov 21 16:07   Sagittarius
Dec 15 12:53   Capricorn

1943

Jan 08 10:03	Aquarius
Feb 01 09:02	Pisces
Feb 25 12:04	Aries
Mar 21 22:24	Taurus
Apr 15 20:12	Gemini
May 11 11:56	Cancer
Jun 07 12:09	Leo
Jul 07 23:56	Virgo
Nov 09 18:25	Libra
Dec 08 07:45	Scorpio

1944

Jan 03 04:43	Sagittarius
Jan 28 03:11	Capricorn
Feb 21 16:40	Aquarius
Mar 17 02:46	Pisces
Apr 10 12:09	Aries
May 04 22:04	Taurus
May 29 08:39	Gemini
Jun 22 19:12	Cancer
Jul 17 04:47	Leo
Aug 10 13:13	Virgo
Sep 03 21:16	Libra
Sep 28 06:12	Scorpio
Oct 22 17:07	Sagittarius
Nov 16 07:26	Capricorn
Dec 11 04:47	Aquarius

1945

Jan 05 19:18	Pisces
Feb 02 08:07	Aries
Mar 11 11:17	Taurus
Apr 07 19:16	Aries

Jun 04 22:58	Taurus
Jul 07 16:20	Gemini
Aug 04 10:59	Cancer
Aug 30 13:05	Leo
Sep 24 16:06	Virgo
Oct 19 04:09	Libra
Nov 12 07:05	Scorpio
Dec 06 05:22	Sagittarius
Dec 30 01:56	Capricorn

1946

Jan 22 22:28	Aquarius
Feb 15 20:11	Pisces
Mar 11 20:32	Aries
Apr 05 01:01	Taurus
Apr 29 10:59	Gemini
May 24 03:39	Cancer
Jun 18 05:00	Leo
Jul 13 19:22	Virgo
Aug 09 08:34	Libra
Sep 07 00:16	Scorpio
Oct 16 10:45	Sagittarius
Nov 08 08:56	Scorpio

1947

Jan 05 16:45	Sagittarius
Feb 06 05:41	Capricorn
Mar 05 05:09	Aquarius
Mar 30 22:14	Pisces
Apr 25 03:03	Aries
May 20 02:06	Taurus
Jun 13 21:35	Gemini
Jul 08 13:30	Cancer
Aug 02 01:06	Leo

Aug 26 08:17	Virgo
Sep 19 12:01	Libra
Oct 13 13:49	Scorpio
Nov 06 14:59	Sagittarius
Nov 30 16:23	Capricorn
Dec 24 19:13	Aquarius

1948

Jan 18 02:14	Pisces
Feb 11 18:51	Aries
Mar 08 06:59	Taurus
Apr 04 12:40	Gemini
May 07 08:27	Cancer
Jun 29 07:58	Gemini
Aug 03 02:15	Cancer
Sep 08 13:40	Leo
Oct 06 12:25	Virgo
Nov 01 06:42	Libra
Nov 26 00:55	Scorpio
Dec 20 07:28	Sagittarius

1949

Jan 13 09:01	Capricorn
Feb 06 09:05	Aquarius
Mar 02 09:38	Pisces
Mar 26 11:54	Aries
Apr 19 16:44	Taurus
May 14 00:25	Gemini
Jun 07 10:47	Cancer
Jul 01 23:40	Leo
Jul 26 15:43	Virgo
Aug 20 12:39	Libra
Sep 14 17:12	Scorpio
Oct 10 10:18	Sagittarius

Nov 06 04:53   Capricorn
Dec 06 06:06   Aquarius

1950

Apr 06 15:13   Pisces
May 05 19:19   Aries
Jun 01 14:19   Taurus
Jun 27 10:45   Gemini
Jul 22 17:50   Cancer
Aug 16 14:18   Leo
Sep 10 01:37   Virgo
Oct 04 05:51   Libra
Oct 28 05:33   Scorpio
Nov 21 03:03   Sagittarius
Dec 14 23:54   Capricorn

1951

Jan 07 21:10   Aquarius
Jan 31 20:14   Pisces
Feb 24 23:26   Aries
Mar 21 10:05   Taurus
Apr 15 08:33   Gemini
May 11 01:41   Cancer
Jun 07 05:10   Leo
Jul 08 04:54   Virgo
Nov 09 18:48   Libra
Dec 08 00:19   Scorpio

1952

Jan 02 18:44   Sagittarius
Jan 27 15:58   Capricorn
Feb 21 04:42   Aquarius
Mar 16 14:18   Pisces
Apr 09 23:17   Aries

May 04 08:55	Taurus
May 28 19:19	Gemini
Jun 22 05:46	Cancer
Jul 16 15:23	Leo
Aug 09 23:58	Virgo
Sep 03 08:17	Libra
Sep 27 17:36	Scorpio
Oct 22 05:02	Sagittarius
Nov 15 20:03	Capricorn
Dec 10 18:30	Aquarius

1953

Jan 05 11:10	Pisces
Feb 02 05:54	Aries
Mar 14 18:58	Taurus
Mar 31 05:17	Aries
Jun 05 10:34	Taurus
Jul 07 10:30	Gemini
Aug 04 01:08	Cancer
Aug 30 01:35	Leo
Sep 24 03:48	Virgo
Oct 18 15:27	Libra
Nov 11 18:12	Scorpio
Dec 05 16:24	Sagittarius
Dec 29 12:53	Capricorn
Jan 22 09:20	Aquarius

1954

Feb 15 07:01	Pisces
Mar 11 07:22	Aries
Apr 04 11:55	Taurus
Apr 28 22:03	Gemini
May 23 15:04	Cancer
Jun 17 17:04	Leo

Jul 13 08:43	Virgo
Aug 09 00:34	Libra
Sep 06 23:29	Scorpio
Oct 23 22:08	Sagittarius
Oct 27 10:42	Scorpio

1955

Jan 06 06:48	Sagittarius
Feb 06 01:15	Capricorn
Mar 04 20:22	Aquarius
Mar 30 11:30	Pisces
Apr 24 15:13	Aries
May 19 13:35	Taurus
Jun 13 08:38	Gemini
Jul 08 00:15	Cancer
Aug 01 11:43	Leo
Aug 25 18:52	Virgo
Sep 18 22:41	Libra
Oct 13 00:39	Scorpio
Nov 06 02:02	Sagittarius
Nov 30 03:42	Capricorn
Dec 24 06:52	Aquarius

1956

Jan 17 14:22	Pisces
Feb 11 07:46	Aries
Mar 07 21:31	Taurus
Apr 04 07:23	Gemini
May 08 02:17	Cancer
Jun 23 12:11	Gemini
Aug 04 09:49	Cancer
Sep 08 09:23	Leo
Oct 06 03:12	Virgo
Oct 31 19:40	Libra

Nov 25 13:01 Scorpio
Dec 19 19:07 Sagittarius

1957
Jan 12 20:23 Capricorn
Feb 05 20:16 Aquarius
Mar 01 20:39 Pisces
Mar 25 22:46 Aries
Apr 19 03:28 Taurus
May 13 11:08 Gemini
Jun 06 21:35 Cancer
Jul 01 10:42 Leo
Jul 26 03:10 Virgo
Aug 20 00:44 Libra
Sep 14 06:20 Scorpio
Oct 10 01:16 Sagittarius
Nov 05 23:46 Capricorn
Dec 06 15:26 Aquarius

1958
Apr 06 16:00 Pisces
May 05 11:59 Aries
Jun 01 04:07 Taurus
Jun 26 23:08 Gemini
Jul 22 05:26 Cancer
Aug 16 01:28 Leo
Sep 09 12:35 Virgo
Oct 03 16:44 Libra
Oct 27 16:26 Scorpio
Nov 20 13:59 Sagittarius
Dec 14 10:55 Capricorn

1959
Jan 07 08:16 Aquarius

Jan 31 07:28	Pisces
Feb 24 10:53	Aries
Mar 20 21:55	Taurus
Apr 14 21:08	Gemini
May 10 15:45	Cancer
Jun 06 22:43	Leo
Jul 08 12:08	Virgo
Sep 20 03:01	Leo
Sep 25 08:15	Virgo
Nov 09 18:11	Libra
Dec 07 16:41	Scorpio

1960

Jan 02 08:43	Sagittarius
Jan 27 04:46	Capricorn
Feb 20 16:47	Aquarius
Mar 16 01:53	Pisces
Apr 09 10:32	Aries
May 03 19:56	Taurus
May 28 06:11	Gemini
Jun 21 16:34	Cancer
Jul 16 02:11	Leo
Aug 09 10:54	Virgo
Sep 02 19:29	Libra
Sep 27 05:13	Scorpio
Oct 21 17:12	Sagittarius
Nov 15 08:57	Capricorn
Dec 10 08:34	Aquarius

1961

Jan 05 03:31	Pisces
Feb 02 04:46	Aries
Jun 05 19:25	Taurus
Jul 07 04:32	Gemini

Aug 03 15:28	Cancer
Aug 29 14:18	Leo
Sep 23 15:43	Virgo
Oct 18 02:58	Libra
Nov 11 05:33	Scorpio
Dec 05 03:40	Sagittarius
Dec 29 00:07	Capricorn

1962

Jan 21 20:31	Aquarius
Feb 14 18:09	Pisces
Mar 10 18:28	Aries
Apr 03 23:05	Taurus
Apr 28 09:23	Gemini
May 23 02:46	Cancer
Jun 17 05:31	Leo
Jul 12 22:32	Virgo
Aug 08 17:13	Libra
Sep 07 00:11	Scorpio

1963

Jan 06 17:35	Sagittarius
Feb 05 20:36	Capricorn
Mar 04 11:41	Aquarius
Mar 30 01:00	Pisces
Apr 24 03:39	Aries
May 19 01:21	Taurus
Jun 12 19:57	Gemini
Jul 07 11:18	Cancer
Jul 31 22:38	Leo
Aug 25 05:49	Virgo
Sep 18 09:43	Libra
Oct 12 11:50	Scorpio
Nov 05 13:25	Sagittarius

Nov 29 15:21	Capricorn
Dec 23 18:53	Aquarius

1964

Jan 17 02:54	Pisces
Feb 10 21:09	Aries
Mar 07 12:38	Taurus
Apr 04 03:03	Gemini
May 09 03:16	Cancer
Jun 17 18:18	Gemini
Aug 05 08:53	Cancer
Sep 08 04:53	Leo
Oct 05 18:10	Virgo
Oct 31 08:54	Libra
Nov 25 01:25	Scorpio
Dec 19 07:02	Sagittarius

1965

Jan 12 08:00	Capricorn
Feb 05 07:41	Aquarius
Mar 01 07:55	Pisces
Mar 25 09:54	Aries
Apr 18 14:31	Taurus
May 12 22:08	Gemini
Jun 06 08:39	Cancer
Jun 30 21:59	Leo
Jul 25 14:51	Virgo
Aug 19 13:06	Libra
Sep 13 19:50	Scorpio
Oct 09 16:46	Sagittarius
Nov 05 19:36	Capricorn
Dec 07 04:37	Aquarius

1966

Feb 06 12:47	Capricorn
Feb 25 10:55	Aquarius
Apr 06 15:53	Pisces
May 05 04:33	Aries
May 31 18:00	Taurus
Jun 26 11:40	Gemini
Jul 21 17:11	Cancer
Aug 15 12:47	Leo
Sep 08 23:40	Virgo
Oct 03 03:44	Libra
Oct 27 03:28	Scorpio
Nov 20 01:06	Sagittarius
Dec 13 22:09	Capricorn

1967

Jan 06 19:36	Aquarius
Jan 30 18:53	Pisces
Feb 23 22:30	Aries
Mar 20 09:56	Taurus
Apr 14 09:54	Gemini
May 10 06:05	Cancer
Jun 06 16:48	Leo
Jul 08 22:11	Virgo
Sep 09 11:58	Leo
Oct 01 18:07	Virgo
Nov 09 16:32	Libra
Dec 07 08:48	Scorpio

1968

Jan 01 22:37	Sagittarius
Jan 26 17:35	Capricorn
Feb 20 04:55	Aquarius
Mar 15 13:32	Pisces

Apr 08 21:48	Aries
May 03 06:56	Taurus
May 27 17:02	Gemini
Jun 21 03:20	Cancer
Jul 15 12:59	Leo
Aug 08 21:49	Virgo
Sep 02 06:39	Libra
Sep 26 16:45	Scorpio
Oct 21 05:16	Sagittarius
Nov 14 21:48	Capricorn
Dec 09 22:40	Aquarius

1969

Jan 04 20:07	Pisces
Feb 02 04:45	Aries
Jun 06 01:48	Taurus
Jul 06 22:04	Gemini
Aug 03 05:30	Cancer
Aug 29 02:48	Leo
Sep 23 03:26	Virgo
Oct 17 14:17	Libra
Nov 10 16:40	Scorpio
Dec 04 14:41	Sagittarius
Dec 28 11:04	Capricorn

1970

Jan 21 07:26	Aquarius
Feb 14 05:04	Pisces
Mar 10 05:25	Aries
Apr 03 10:05	Taurus
Apr 27 20:33	Gemini
May 22 14:19	Cancer
Jun 16 17:49	Leo
Jul 12 12:16	Virgo

| Aug 08 09:59 | Libra |
| Sep 07 01:54 | Scorpio |

1971

Jan 07 01:00	Sagittarius
Feb 05 14:57	Capricorn
Mar 04 02:24	Aquarius
Mar 29 14:02	Pisces
Apr 23 15:44	Aries
May 18 12:48	Taurus
Jun 12 06:58	Gemini
Jul 06 22:02	Cancer
Jul 31 09:15	Leo
Aug 24 16:25	Virgo
Sep 17 20:25	Libra
Oct 11 22:43	Scorpio
Nov 05 00:30	Sagittarius
Nov 29 02:41	Capricorn
Dec 23 06:32	Aquarius

1972

Jan 16 15:01	Pisces
Feb 10 10:08	Aries
Mar 07 03:25	Taurus
Apr 03 22:48	Gemini
May 10 13:51	Cancer
Jun 11 20:09	Gemini
Aug 06 01:26	Cancer
Sep 07 23:27	Leo
Oct 05 08:33	Virgo
Oct 30 21:40	Libra
Nov 24 13:23	Scorpio
Dec 18 18:34	Sagittarius

1973

Jan 11 19:15	Capricorn
Feb 04 18:43	Aquarius
Feb 28 18:45	Pisces
Mar 24 20:34	Aries
Apr 18 01:05	Taurus
May 12 08:42	Gemini
Jun 05 19:20	Cancer
Jun 30 08:55	Leo
Jul 25 02:13	Virgo
Aug 19 01:10	Libra
Sep 13 09:05	Scorpio
Oct 09 08:08	Sagittarius
Nov 05 15:39	Capricorn
Dec 07 21:37	Aquarius

1974

Jan 29 19:51	Capricorn
Feb 28 14:25	Aquarius
Apr 06 14:17	Pisces
May 04 20:21	Aries
May 31 07:19	Taurus
Jun 25 23:44	Gemini
Jul 21 04:34	Cancer
Aug 14 23:47	Leo
Sep 08 10:28	Virgo
Oct 02 14:27	Libra
Oct 26 14:12	Scorpio
Nov 19 11:56	Sagittarius
Dec 13 09:06	Capricorn

1975

Jan 06 06:39	Aquarius
Jan 30 06:05	Pisces

Feb 23 09:53	Aries
Mar 19 21:42	Taurus
Apr 13 22:26	Gemini
May 09 20:11	Cancer
Jun 06 10:54	Leo
Jul 09 11:06	Virgo
Sep 02 15:34	Leo
Oct 04 05:20	Virgo
Nov 09 13:52	Libra
Dec 07 00:29	Scorpio

1976

Jan 01 12:14	Sagittarius
Jan 26 06:09	Capricorn
Feb 19 16:50	Aquarius
Mar 15 00:59	Pisces
Apr 08 08:56	Aries
May 02 17:49	Taurus
May 27 03:43	Gemini
Jun 20 13:56	Cancer
Jul 14 23:36	Leo
Aug 08 08:36	Virgo
Sep 01 17:44	Libra
Sep 26 04:17	Scorpio
Oct 20 17:22	Sagittarius
Nov 14 10:42	Capricorn
Dec 09 12:53	Aquarius

1977

Jan 04 13:01	Pisces
Feb 02 05:54	Aries
Jun 06 06:10	Taurus
Jul 06 15:09	Gemini
Aug 02 19:19	Cancer

Aug 28 15:09	Leo
Sep 22 15:05	Virgo
Oct 17 01:37	Libra
Nov 10 03:52	Scorpio
Dec 04 01:49	Sagittarius
Dec 27 22:09	Capricorn
Jan 20 18:29	Aquarius

1978

Feb 13 16:07	Pisces
Mar 09 16:29	Aries
Apr 02 21:14	Taurus
Apr 27 07:53	Gemini
May 22 02:03	Cancer
Jun 16 06:19	Leo
Jul 12 02:14	Virgo
Aug 08 03:08	Libra
Sep 07 05:07	Scorpio

1979

Jan 07 06:38	Sagittarius
Feb 05 09:16	Capricorn
Mar 03 17:18	Aquarius
Mar 29 03:18	Pisces
Apr 23 04:02	Aries
May 18 00:29	Taurus
Jun 11 18:13	Gemini
Jul 06 09:02	Cancer
Jul 30 20:07	Leo
Aug 24 03:16	Virgo
Sep 17 07:21	Libra
Oct 11 09:48	Scorpio
Nov 04 11:50	Sagittarius
Nov 28 14:20	Capricorn

Dec 22 18:35   Aquarius

1980

Jan 16 03:37   Pisces
Feb 09 23:39   Aries
Mar 06 18:54   Taurus
Apr 03 19:46   Gemini
May 12 20:53   Cancer
Jun 05 05:44   Gemini
Aug 06 14:25   Cancer
Sep 07 17:57   Leo
Oct 04 23:07   Virgo
Oct 30 10:38   Libra
Nov 24 01:35   Scorpio
Dec 18 06:21   Sagittarius

1981

Jan 11 06:48   Capricorn
Feb 04 06:07   Aquarius
Feb 28 06:01   Pisces
Mar 24 07:43   Aries
Apr 17 12:08   Taurus
May 11 19:45   Gemini
Jun 05 06:29   Cancer
Jun 29 20:20   Leo
Jul 24 14:04   Virgo
Aug 18 13:44   Libra
Sep 12 22:51   Scorpio
Oct 09 00:04   Sagittarius
Nov 05 12:39   Capricorn
Dec 08 20:53   Aquarius

1982

Jan 23 02:56 30 Capricorn

Mar 02 11:25	Aquarius
Apr 06 12:20	Pisces
May 04 12:27	Aries
May 30 21:02	Taurus
Jun 25 12:13	Gemini
Jul 20 16:21	Cancer
Aug 14 11:09	Leo
Sep 07 21:38	Virgo
Oct 02 01:32	Libra
Oct 26 01:19	Scorpio
Nov 18 23:07	Sagittarius
Dec 12 20:20	Capricorn

1983

Jan 05 17:58	Aquarius
Jan 29 17:31	Pisces
Feb 22 21:35	Aries
Mar 19 09:51	Taurus
Apr 13 11:26	Gemini
May 09 10:56	Cancer
Jun 06 06:04	Leo
Jul 10 05:25	Virgo
Aug 27 11:44	Leo
Oct 05 19:35	Virgo
Nov 09 10:52	Libra
Dec 06 16:15	Scorpio

1984

Jan 01 02:00	Sagittarius
Jan 25 18:51	Capricorn
Feb 19 04:53	Aquarius
Mar 14 12:35	Pisces
Apr 07 20:13	Aries
May 02 04:53	Taurus

May 26 14:40	Gemini
Jun 20 00:48	Cancer
Jul 14 10:30	Leo
Aug 07 19:40	Virgo
Sep 01 05:07	Libra
Sep 25 16:05	Scorpio
Oct 20 05:45	Sagittarius
Nov 13 23:54	Capricorn
Dec 09 03:26	Aquarius

1985

Jan 04 06:23	Pisces
Feb 02 08:29	Aries
Jun 06 08:53	Taurus
Jul 06 08:01	Gemini
Aug 02 09:10	Cancer
Aug 28 03:39	Leo
Sep 22 02:53	Virgo
Oct 16 13:04	Libra
Nov 09 15:08	Scorpio
Dec 03 13:00	Sagittarius
Dec 27 09:17	Capricorn

1986

Jan 20 05:36	Aquarius
Feb 13 03:11	Pisces
Mar 09 03:32	Aries
Apr 02 08:19	Taurus
Apr 26 19:10	Gemini
May 21 13:46	Cancer
Jun 15 18:52	Leo
Jul 11 16:23	Virgo
Aug 07 20:46	Libra
Sep 07 10:15	Scorpio

1987

Jan 07 10:20	Sagittarius
Feb 05 03:03	Capricorn
Mar 03 07:55	Aquarius
Mar 28 16:20	Pisces
Apr 22 16:07	Aries
May 17 11:56	Taurus
Jun 11 05:15	Gemini
Jul 05 19:50	Cancer
Jul 30 06:49	Leo
Aug 23 14:00	Virgo
Sep 16 18:12	Libra
Oct 10 20:49	Scorpio
Nov 03 23:04	Sagittarius
Nov 28 01:51	Capricorn
Dec 22 06:29	Aquarius

1988

Jan 15 16:04	Pisces
Feb 09 13:04	Aries
Mar 06 10:21	Taurus
Apr 03 17:07	Gemini
May 17 16:27	Cancer
May 27 07:36	Gemini
Aug 06 23:24	Cancer
Sep 07 11:37	Leo
Oct 04 13:15	Virgo
Oct 29 23:20	Libra
Nov 23 13:34	Scorpio
Dec 17 17:56	Sagittarius

1989

Jan 10 18:08	Capricorn
Feb 03 17:15	Aquarius

Feb 27 16:59	Pisces
Mar 23 18:32	Aries
Apr 16 22:52	Taurus
May 11 06:28	Gemini
Jun 04 17:17	Cancer
Jun 29 07:21	Leo
Jul 24 01:31	Virgo
Aug 18 01:58	Libra
Sep 12 12:22	Scorpio
Oct 08 16:00	Sagittarius
Nov 05 10:13	Capricorn
Dec 10 04:54	Aquarius

1990

Jan 16 15:24	Capricorn
Mar 03 17:52	Aquarius
Apr 06 09:13	Pisces
May 04 03:52	Aries
May 30 10:13	Taurus
Jun 25 00:14	Gemini
Jul 20 03:41	Cancer
Aug 13 22:05	Leo
Sep 07 08:21	Virgo
Oct 01 12:13	Libra
Oct 25 12:03	Scorpio
Nov 18 09:58	Sagittarius
Dec 12 07:18	Capricorn

1991

Jan 05 05:03	Aquarius
Jan 29 04:44	Pisces
Feb 22 09:02	Aries
Mar 18 21:45	Taurus
Apr 13 00:10	Gemini

May 09 01:28	Cancer
Jun 06 01:16	Leo
Jul 11 05:06	Virgo
Aug 21 15:06	Leo
Oct 06 21:15	Virgo
Nov 09 06:37	Libra
Dec 06 07:21	Scorpio
Dec 31 15:19	Sagittarius

1992

Jan 25 07:14	Capricorn
Feb 18 16:40	Aquarius
Mar 13 23:57	Pisces
Apr 07 07:16	Aries
May 01 15:41	Taurus
May 26 01:18	Gemini
Jun 19 11:22	Cancer
Jul 13 21:07	Leo
Aug 07 06:26	Virgo
Aug 31 16:09	Libra
Sep 25 03:31	Scorpio
Oct 19 17:47	Sagittarius
Nov 13 12:48	Capricorn
Dec 08 17:49	Aquarius

1993

Jan 03 23:54	Pisces
Feb 02 12:37	Aries
Jun 06 10:03	Taurus
Jul 06 00:21	Gemini
Aug 01 22:38	Cancer
Aug 27 15:48	Leo
Sep 21 14:22	Virgo
Oct 16 00:13	Libra

Nov 09 02:07   Scorpio
Dec 02 23:54   Sagittarius
Dec 26 20:09   Capricorn

1994

Jan 19 16:28   Aquarius
Feb 12 14:04   Pisces
Mar 08 14:28   Aries
Apr 01 19:20   Taurus
Apr 26 06:24   Gemini
May 21 01:26   Cancer
Jun 15 07:23   Leo
Jul 11 06:33   Virgo
Aug 07 14:36   Libra
Sep 07 17:12   Scorpio

1995

Jan 07 12:07   Sagittarius
Feb 04 20:12   Capricorn
Mar 02 22:10   Aquarius
Mar 28 05:10   Pisces
Apr 22 04:07   Aries
May 16 23:22   Taurus
Jun 10 16:18   Gemini
Jul 05 06:39   Cancer
Jul 29 17:32   Leo
Aug 23 00:43   Virgo
Sep 16 05:01   Libra
Oct 10 07:48   Scorpio
Nov 03 10:18   Sagittarius
Nov 27 13:23   Capricorn
Dec 21 18:23   Aquarius

1996

Jan 15 04:30	Pisces
Feb 09 02:30	Aries
Mar 06 02:01	Taurus
Apr 03 15:26	Gemini
Aug 07 06:15	Cancer
Sep 07 05:07	Leo
Oct 04 03:22	Virgo
Oct 29 12:02	Libra
Nov 23 01:34	Scorpio
Dec 17 05:34	Sagittarius

1997

Jan 10 05:32	Capricorn
Feb 03 04:28	Aquarius
Feb 27 04:01	Pisces
Mar 23 05:26	Aries
Apr 16 09:43	Taurus
May 10 17:20	Gemini
Jun 04 04:18	Cancer
Jun 28 18:38	Leo
Jul 23 13:16	Virgo
Aug 17 14:31	Libra
Sep 12 02:17	Scorpio
Oct 08 08:25	Sagittarius
Nov 05 08:50	Capricorn
Dec 12 04:39	Aquarius

1998

Jan 09 21:04	Capricorn
Mar 04 16:14	Aquarius
Apr 06 05:38	Pisces
May 03 19:16	Aries
May 29 23:32	Taurus

Jun 24 12:27	Gemini
Jul 19 15:17	Cancer
Aug 13 09:19	Leo
Sep 06 19:24	Virgo
Sep 30 23:13	Libra
Oct 24 23:06	Scorpio
Nov 17 21:06	Sagittarius
Dec 11 18:33	Capricorn

1999

Jan 04 16:25	Aquarius
Jan 28 16:17	Pisces
Feb 21 20:49	Aries
Mar 18 09:59	Taurus
Apr 12 13:17	Gemini
May 08 16:29	Cancer
Jun 05 21:25	Leo
Jul 12 15:18	Virgo
Aug 15 14:12	Leo
Oct 07 16:51	Virgo
Nov 09 02:19	Libra
Dec 05 22:41	Scorpio
Dec 31 04:54	Sagittarius

2000

Jan 24 19:52	Capricorn
Feb 18 04:43	Aquarius
Mar 13 11:36	Pisces
Apr 06 18:37	Aries
May 01 02:49	Taurus
May 25 12:15	Gemini
Jun 18 22:15	Cancer
Jul 13 08:02	Leo
Aug 06 17:32	Virgo

Aug 31 03:35   Libra
Sep 24 15:26   Scorpio
Oct 19 06:18   Sagittarius
Nov 13 02:14   Capricorn
Dec 08 08:48   Aquarius

Chapter 14

Who to Love if You Have Venus in Aries

If you have Venus in Aries you often let your heart rule your head. You fall in love quickly and tend to want things to follow through to their passionate conclusion sooner rather than later as you want to know exactly what you're getting into, fast! No long, drawn-out dates or lengthy engagements for you.

Sometimes you're in danger of falling in love with the high that you get from being in love, but being unable to sustain that feeling is what can lead you to have a succession of flings rather than a long-term, real thing.

So what are the key ingredients for your Mr. Right? You, more than most signs, respond to physical attractiveness. Aries relates to the head and face so you'll be strongly drawn to someone who you think looks good, or even has that odd but alluring blend of handsome-ugly going on (think Gerard Depardieu).

He certainly needs to have a masculine quality about him, as you too can be upfront when it comes to passion so you need someone who can communicate and express his needs and desires on the same level as you.

He could be someone who works in a competitive environment, anything from sales to sport to running his own business. He always likes to come first and be the top dog so ideally you're looking for an Alpha male.

He's at the sharp end of business, possibly literally as Aries is connected to sharp objects so he could be a surgeon, a tree surgeon or knife thrower at the circus, but don't discount your local butcher or even someone who owns a specialist knife shop or who supplies equipment to chefs.

Sports-wise he could be into fencing, archery or throwing the javelin. But he also needs and loves to express his masculinity through macho exploits like karate, kickboxing and clay-pigeon shooting.

If you're sporty yourself you could always sign up for a course in any of these to meet the man of your dreams, or join a military fitness program as Aries is ruled by Mars, the warrior planet, and a well-honed instructor could put you through your paces and capture your heart at the same time if you're lucky.

Venus in Aries loves warmth and heat so you could find him on a vacation in the sunshine or at a bonfire party. Also look for him where there are one-off events or premieres as this combo makes you and the man you're in search of love to be first in line for the latest book, film, gadget or nightclub so you can both show off to friends and family who haven't yet had the experience.

If you like the good things in life you're doubly blessed as the man you seek attracts money and likes the signs of his success to be on display. He'll want you to look good on his arm. Nothing but the best will do for him and frankly you will be the best as far as he's concerned, so he'll share his riches with you without hesitation.

This is the Venus combination that indicates a tendency towards love and lust at first sight. Just take a little more time to make sure your relationship can build to an eternal flame, not blow out like a candle.

So let's keep this simple and create a list of options that you can add to your master plan at the back of the book so you can identify him when you meet him. Your love match could be:

- A fireman
- An acupuncturist
- A firearms expert
- An entrepreneur
- A surgeon
- A boxer

- A company director
- A racing driver
- A military man
- A glass blower
- A pizza maker
- A leader in his field
- A blacksmith
- A film director
- A tango dancer

This list is by no means exhaustive and you can, and should, add some options of your own. You should be getting the picture by now. Think of the things you admire that include any form of heat, an adrenaline rush, action, being first or being in charge and that's the kind of lover you should be drawing towards you, or putting yourself in a position to get closer to.

Which House is Your Venus in Aries Sign In?

The astrological house that your Venus sign is in tells you even more about your ideal love match. If you haven't done it already, look back at the 'Find your Venus Sign' chapter for a quick and easy way to work it out.

First house: He's drop dead gorgeous in a very masculine way. He might have red hair or perhaps have a scar on his face. He knows how to make an entrance, be seen at all the right places and spends his money on sharp suits worn with a 'couldn't care less' attitude. He's trouble but he's worth it.

Second house: He's a money maker, driven to succeed and motivated by cash, which elevates his self esteem. While he loves to make money he also loves to spend it, so he's likely to be very generous, showering you with expensive gifts, that must-have handbag or that limited edition piece of jewelry.

Third house: This one loves to be at the cutting edge of news, so you'll find him browsing the newspapers or on his laptop in a coffee shop accessing whatever's going on in the world. He likes to be first with information so he's the go-to guy to find out what's going on in the media, at work or in your neighborhood.

Fourth house: Venus in Aries here is a fast food fan. He needs to refuel often and quickly, but may be a bit of a Gordon Ramsay (fiery and bossy) in the kitchen and is sure to be king of the barbecue in the summer so don't interfere as that's totally his domain. His bedroom is likely to be bold and masculine with red or black satin sheets as he loves to mix comfort with passion and drama.

Fifth house: If you're the possessive type beware, as this guy will keep you on your toes. It's his mission in life to get as many women's phone numbers as possible and even if he's attached he won't be able to stop flirting. If you're made of strong stuff you could find this a challenge and a turn on. He'll always come home to you but likes the thrill of a conquest elsewhere, without necessarily following through.

Sixth house: He's likely to wear out the mirrors in your home through checking out his own reflection. That said, he really does take care of himself at the gym and in later years won't be averse to going under the knife to keep the aging process at bay. Healthy food and a fit lifestyle are his passions and he'll insist that you follow suit. He might also have a pet that he's crazy about.

Seventh house: This is the realm of the macho man who wants to take care of his woman in very traditional ways. You'll be put on a pedestal and be expected to make him proud when you're out in public together and be the perfect housewife at home, though he'll respect you for having your own career too.

Eighth house: He's a lady-killer, a demon and a delight between the sheets and a master of the art of seduction. He's the epitome of tall, dark and handsome, and even if he doesn't actually look that way, that's the vibe he'll give out. Masterful and very good with money, he's also secretive and mysterious about that and just about everything else too, which only adds to the attraction.

Ninth house: This one loves adventure. Think of intrepid explorers like Bear Grylls or Indiana Jones. He's never happier than when pioneering through uncharted territory so he could be a traveler, explorer or even a missionary as he's rather spiritual too. Nothing wears him down or tires him out and he's got a great sense of humor.

Tenth house: He's the boss, or at the very least the boss's wingman with aspirations. More likely, he'll run his own business, if not now then soon, and he'll be exceptionally astute where cash and investments are concerned. He has an air of poise, calm and sophistication about him but you wouldn't want to cross him. He's a man who's going places and intends to travel there first class.

Eleventh house: He's the mover and shaker amongst his friends and associates. He knows the best places to go, especially where there are new openings and first nights, and will get you in on the guest list so you'll feel like you're getting exclusive red carpet treatment.

Twelfth house: With twelfth house Venus in Aries, things are less obvious. Signs and signals are subliminal so you'll be love-struck without even knowing he's been aiming his arrows at your heart. He's the strong, silent type who says little but his words carry weight. The undercover boss, the unassuming millionaire perhaps. There's more to him than meets the eye and he's worth getting to know, though beware that deep down he may still be stuck on his first love.

Chapter 15

Who to Love if You Have Venus in Taurus

Every girl's crazy about a sharp-dressed man, aren't they? There's a strong chance that you will be if you have Venus in Taurus. Think Armani suits, leather shoes, a guy who looks great in a simple white t-shirt and blue jeans, and who smells divine.

He's also incredibly tactile and loves to stroke your hair and put his arm around your waist.

If you hadn't realized it before, this is the kind of man you should be looking for. You have a taste for the finer things in life, quality as opposed to quantity, although if there's something you like, whether it's exquisite food or divine kissing, you often can't get enough of it as Venus in Taurus stimulates your sensuality and your sense of entitlement too.

So when you're looking for love it's important that you find someone who makes you feel valued. This can be through gifts and tokens of affection, and they don't have to be worth a fortune but they do have to be things that support how you feel about yourself.

For instance, a giant bottle of cheap perfume, no matter how showy, means less to you than a small phial of exquisitely wrapped, deliciously scented body oil. A massive bouquet of clashing colored, gas station flowers will appall you, as you'd sooner have a handful of dark, velvety roses tied with a silk ribbon. And a picnic in the countryside is perfect but with goat's cheese tartlets, homemade lemonade and a handmade truffle or two for dessert, not a thrown together ragbag of convenience store sandwiches, sodas and plastic-tasting candy bars.

Likewise you flourish through touch, little signs of affection to show that you're connected to the one you love. Random kisses and affectionate caresses make you feel needed and wanted, more than you realize. You're a sensual creature who needs to be loved. Don't we all, but you in particular need tangible proof of that fact, and are more than willing to reciprocate.

The kind of man who will be there for you in ways that you need is quite an earthy type, but he also appreciates style, sensuality, warmth, consistency and quality. You could find him in an art gallery or at an exhibition, he could be a collector of antiques and he loves to eat so foodie hangouts are a good haunt if you want to track him down.

Music soothes his soul, particularly the sultry tones of a skilled singer who has the power to move him. If he comes back to your place after a date, set the mood with music to seduce and be seduced by, so there's no confusing the message you're sending and he'll respond as required.

Being out in nature is also good for you and could be a great place to meet your match too. Long country walks, heritage homes with amazing gardens and fabulously ornate but tasteful decor may well appeal to you and he'll appreciate these things too (up to a point).

Classic car and motorbike rallies and outdoors antiques markets are his hunting grounds and should also become yours during the summer weekends, and you can seek him out at farmers markets and agricultural shows too.

If none of these sound like your kind of thing, then think about the things you do love to do that connect you with Venus in Taurus. You do them already in some shape or form so think outdoorsy, arty, earthy. It could be a crazy music festival where you're up to your boots in mud. Follow what you love doing and love will follow you.

And while he could very well be a stylish man of means, he could also be incredibly down to earth with a very basic sense of humor. He might be a guy who's perhaps a little rough around the edges but with a heart of gold and a true desire for permanence within a relationship, something that will certainly appeal to your sense of stability in this ever-changing and unpredictable world.

And you can practically guarantee that he'll demonstrate his affections without fail in bed, or outdoors, or wherever the mood strikes. Plus you'll always have food on the table and a secure roof over your head with this guy.

So let's keep this simple and create a list of options that you can add to your master plan at the back of the book so you can identify him when you meet him. Your love match could be:

- A farmer
- A banker
- A florist
- A chef
- A masseur
- A gardener
- A singer
- A real estate agent
- An interior designer
- A jeweler
- A chocolatier
- A restaurant owner
- A clothes designer
- A landlord
- A wine merchant

This list is by no means exhaustive and you can, and should, add some options of your own. You should be getting the picture by now. Think of the things you adore that include any form of luxury, comfort, style, quality, sensuality, classic things that are made to last, and being in touch with nature and that's the kind of lover you should be drawing towards you, or putting yourself in a position to get closer to.

Which House is Your Venus in Taurus Sign In?

The astrological house that your Venus sign is in tells you even more about your ideal love match. If you haven't done it already, look back at the 'Find your Venus Sign' chapter for a quick and easy way to work it out.

First house: He's attractive as hell, and smells good too, almost reminiscent of the best things that money can buy: Good leather, Sicilian lemons, tropical sunshine. He's solid, has a steady gaze, and dresses to impress so that even if he's kind of scruffy he'll still look smart. A little bit narcissistic, but irresistible nonetheless.

Second house: There's an aura of quality about this guy. You'll want to stroke his clothes, as they may be vintage but they'll be soft and classic, as will he. He likes to touch things before he gives them space in his life so expect a very tactile experience with him. Banking, wealth, antiques and investments are his thing, and he likes to invest in relationships too so he's definitely a keeper.

Third house: A singer, a poet, a playwright, a speaker with a lovely voice. He could recite the phone book (ideally in Italian, sigh!) and you'll be happy to hang on his every word. He might be a writer of cookery books or songs, as words and the way he uses them are his currency.

Fourth house: You'll never starve with this man as he loves food and will love to feed you, possibly to excess so beware if you tend to pile on the pounds. Not that he will mind as he's probably a little on the solid side himself. He likes to taste and savor life and will be an excellent kisser, and is also likely to have a sumptuous home.

Fifth house: He likes to tease, tempt and flirt, and he does it with such charm you can't help but fall for him. He's also a lot of fun as romance is his hobby and his passion. He'll take you to music gigs, to the theater and to romantic restaurants. This man is in love with love so expect a lifetime of dating with him, even after you get hitched.

Sixth house: This one looks after his body, but not in a showy way. He'll be neat and tidy, well groomed at all times, and fit too but more from digging in his garden or physical hard work than strutting about in the gym. He'll love country walks and could be a something of an eco warrior. The smell of a freshly tilled field or a new mown lawn are aphrodisiacs to him.

Seventh house: He's a bit of a traditionalist and wants, when the time is right, the whole white wedding thing. He's loyal, faithful, adorable, dependable and expects you to be the same or there will be big trouble. Do not make him jealous under any circumstances. He's solid in all his connections, including business where he has a reputation for fairness and a skill with moneymaking.

Eighth house: He's sexy and he knows it. And you will too. The thrill of contemplating ending up horizontal with this man can make you lose control, but it'll be worth it. He has a presence that reeks of power, and he may be quite secretive about how he makes his money, but it could be that it's from waste disposal rather than something more glamorous and he doesn't want his sultry image tarnished. He might be guarded, but it's not because he's keeping secrets from you, he just has issues with trust. Be trustworthy and he's yours for life.

Ninth house: He could be a scholar but more likely a lecturer as his passion is to share his philosophy of life with the world, and he has a mesmerizing voice with which to do it. He loves to learn, and to share wisdom, and he's probably traveled the world in style, or will do with you. Spot him by his timeless tweed jacket, or the well-worn motorbike leathers as he takes you for a spin on his classic Triumph, to the countryside or to lunch at a university town.

Tenth house: He's the boss of wherever he works, or will be soon. He makes money for a company that's stable and secure, possibly manufacturing quality goods such as food, chocolates, clothes or farming implements, or he's the sexiest bank manager in the world. He exudes power, and the subtle scent of good aftershave. He sticks to his guns and can be quite stubborn as he likes what he knows and knows what he likes.

Eleventh house: This man makes his dreams come true through persistence and through his friends and connections. He's probably known his friends since childhood and intends to keep it that way. Get in with them and you'll be part of his inner circle too as they're an extension of his personality and his lifestyle. His dreams include a world where everyone gets on, money is shared, beauty is all around and he'll roll up his sleeves and pitch in to help his vision become a reality. He may live in a commune or share his house with others.

Twelfth house: He's a romantic dreamer whose idea of love is old-time movie star glamour, and he'll treat you like his leading lady. He may expect you to rescue him from the hardships of reality at times so you'll need to be made of tough stuff to support his fantasies, but he'll merge with your heart and soul forever.

Chapter 16

Who to Love if You Have Venus in Gemini

If you've ever trawled through internet dating sites or perused newspaper adverts seeking a soulmate you'll know the shorthand GSOH, and a Good Sense Of Humor is something your love interest will definitely need to keep you amused and enthralled.

In fact the internet is one of the best places for you in particular to find a partner, as having Venus in Gemini means you have a real love of communication in all its forms.

With Venus here you need to have your mind stimulated as well as your heart. You love to talk, you like to know what's going on, to share news and information and, on occasion, you may like to hear and divulge a little bit of gossip. You can't bear to be kept out of the loop or to feel that you're not being listened to so the strong, silent type is not for you.

When you're looking for love, then, you need someone who can communicate on your level. Too highbrow and you'll feel frustrated, too lowbrow and you'll be bored. You can also be quite flirtatious and a good pick-up line that's smart and sassy rather than cheesy (though that can depend on your ever-changing moods) will capture your attention and potentially win your heart.

That's not to say you'll be bowled over by someone who's a motormouth, but anyone who appreciates words is certainly worth some investment of your time.

The chances are you already do something, somewhere in your life, that connects with your Venus in Gemini. It's what you love to do so you must do it in some shape or form simply to enjoy your existence.

It could be that you write poetry or love reading books.

Perhaps you've even thought about writing a book. The person of your dreams enjoys these things too, or embodies them in some way.

He could be a journalist, a songwriter or a poet. He could be the cute, available English teacher at your child's school, or the tutor at a creative writing course you attend, as Venus in Gemini shows that you love to learn and to share your knowledge. Taking a class or even teaching a class could put you in touch with someone who suits you perfectly. It doesn't have to be about writing, as sharing any skill you have places you in the right zone.

If you're true to your Venus in Gemini sign, you're likely to love all forms of communication so your heart's desire could work at the library or at your favorite book store. If he's there it's probably because he loves those things too so if you make a point of asking for advice or recommendations you've created an opening for you both to talk about your specialist subject. Result!

This astrological combination is also about travel so if you love to drive or enjoy whatever means of transport you use to get around, make the most of it. Venus in Gemini can help you find love on your regular commute on the bus, on a bike ride, or on a train journey to a vacation destination (more so than on a long haul journey by air). Don't be afraid to strike up a conversation with that intriguing guy sitting next to you, although with Venus in Gemini it's unlikely that you'll feel tongue-tied about making the first move and chances are he'll love to talk and listen as much as you do.

You'll also particularly appreciate anyone with a lovely voice. Whether speaking or singing, a gorgeous voice will make you melt, so make sure you listen out as you may well hear your future love before you actually see him.

So let's keep this simple and create a list of options that you can add to your master plan at the back of the book so you can identify him when you meet him. Your love match could be:

- A writer
- A poet
- A teacher, especially of English or a foreign language
- A bookseller
- An IT specialist
- An advertising salesperson
- A tour guide or travel representative
- A car salesperson
- A storyteller
- A quiz setter
- A comedian
- Someone who drives, either for a living or as a serious pleasure
- A car valet
- A singer or songwriter
- A ticket inspector

This list is by no means exhaustive and you can, and should, add some options of your own. You should be getting the picture by now. Think of the things you adore that include any form of communication or travel, words, books, phones, gossip, news, quick wit and information and that's the kind of lover you should be drawing towards you, or putting yourself in a position to get closer to.

Which House is Your Venus in Gemini Sign In?

The astrological house that your Venus sign is in tells you even more about your ideal love match. If you haven't done it already, look back at the 'Find your Venus Sign' chapter for a quick and easy way to work it out.

First house: He's very fashionable, with an extremely expressive face. A raised eyebrow speaks volumes, and his body language is very revealing, plus he can read yours like a book. You might find this guy loves to talk about himself rather a lot but he'll be so fascinating you'll be hanging on every word.

Second house: Your love match is good with money and is a bit of a wheeler-dealer who enjoys a good bargain hunt and to haggle. Money flows in and out but there's always enough and sometimes more than enough to get by on and live the good life.

Third house: Your lover is likely to be a teacher, a writer on a local newspaper or works with transport in some way. He may write a travel newsletter or work in local government, perhaps as a spokesperson for local issues, and he loves to talk about putting the world to rights.

Fourth house: He may write about food, even if it's just getting creative with the menus on the blackboard at your local bar or café. He'll copy, collect or invent recipes too. Family issues are also important so expect lots of communication with relatives and trips to visit his extended family.

Fifth house: An incorrigible flirt with the gift of the gab, your love match is very creative and most likely a bit of a show off. He could be a children's entertainer or actor. He loves gossip and is in the know about what's going on where, knows all the story lines to all the TV soaps and all about celebrity lifestyles too.

Sixth house: You'll find the object of your desire working out at the gym or shopping at the health food store. He'll be into the body beautiful, yours as well as his, and is a treasure trove of information about well-being. He's likely to be supremely organized and love filing and alphabetizing his books, CDs and DVDs, so much so that he may seem a little OCD. You'll know him by the shine on his car, and it will be spotless.

Seventh house: This is one of those rare men who loves to talk about relationships, where things are going, how you're feeling and how he's feeling about how you're feeling. He communicates brilliantly with others, which makes him extremely attractive but do beware of jealousy as he spreads his attention rather thinly at times. That doesn't mean you're not the most important person in his life, so long as you remain endlessly fascinating.

Eighth house: He's an investigative journalist, perhaps a spy. He may be a sex therapist. He prefers to listen rather than talk and will encourage you to reveal all your secrets without giving away too many of his own, plus he'll be extremely inventive between the sheets. He could be into high finance and has a brilliant but devious mind.

Ninth house: Travel and spirituality rule this one. He's a professor, possibly from overseas or is someone who's able to speak several languages. He has a great sense of humor and may even be a successful stand-up comedian. He's a deep thinker and adventurer who loves to learn as much as he can about the world around him. He could also be a media mogul or super-smooth advertising salesman.

Tenth house: He's an entrepreneur with fingers in lots of pies. For him, work is like spinning plates, an intellectual experience, but he takes it very seriously and wants to be taken seriously too. He has the ability to make a lot of money and to be recognized and rewarded for his achievements so may be a workaholic.

Eleventh house: He loves his friends and is most likely to be found in a group of pals. Work-wise he could be involved in some kind of co-operative or fraternal organization. He enjoys all things alternative, may be a bit of a hippy or have unusual ideas about love and life, and is extremely generous to his friends with his time and his resources.

Twelfth house: He's something of a romantic hero: More of a Romeo than a swashbuckler or knight in shining armor, but he will want to rescue you in some way. He might drive an ambulance or be a vehicle breakdown recovery man. He could be a counselor, a poet, a singer or dancer, and is a gentle type who'll want to merge with you in mind, body and soul.

Chapter 17

Who to Love if You Have Venus in Cancer

No matter what your Sun sign is, whether you're go-getting, sexy or a dreamer, the one thing you truly seem to love with Venus in Cancer is your home. More specifically, the home and possible family that you hope to have with the right guy someday soon.

Venus in Cancer shows that you relish and romanticize your home-life. Where you live is likely to be a complete comfort-fest, festooned with plumped up throw pillows and the coziest furnishings you can find. A well-stocked kitchen full of temping yet wholesome treats turns your home into a nest that it would seem foolish to ever want to leave.

You want someone to look after, and you'll do it superbly, but the truth is you also want someone to look after you. Not in a sad, lost little girl kind of way, but in a traditional, loving protective way that makes you feel secure and stable but strong too. No one will fight harder to defend their home and loved ones than you, should they happen to be under threat in any way. At such times you're a tigress not a kitten.

And the kind of guy you're looking for also feels that home is where his heart is. He's the type who likes to fix things up around the house. Even if he's useless at DIY he'll have a vision of how home should be and will happily pay for an expert to come and sort out domestic glitches and make his (and your) surroundings beautiful, comfortable but practical too. He probably likes to cook, which is always an attractive quality in a man, and almost undoubtedly will be good with children, his, yours or anyone else's.

The one thing he truly needs is to feel that his efforts are appreciated and he will sulk if he doesn't get the kind of attention he believes his input deserves. Expect him to go into an almost impenetrable shell and put up defenses that only the most ardent coaxing and temptations of massages, meals and more will lure him out of, eventually. He might forgive but he won't forget a slight, so keeping the peace is important with this guy.

So where do you find him? Venus in Cancer is all about what you love and what you love to do, so there's a chance that your paths will cross in the food aisles of your local supermarket, as you both may be foodies on the quiet, or at a DIY store or furnishing outlet as you both like to feather your nests. He could be the owner of a grandiose home, or be a dreamy real estate agent showing you around your perfect home. You could even meet on a cookery course.

There's a strong likelihood that you'll both be drawn to water, so you could encounter him while walking your dog on a beach or by the river. If you like sailing, hang out at yacht clubs as he may have money as well as a passion for boats. Not that you're a gold-digger, but security is extremely important to your emotional as well as your physical well-being. Heck, if he's happy to pay to take you on a rowing boat around the lake in the park you'll most likely be happy too, because another thing you'll share in common with your ideal man is an almost telepathic connection about each other's needs, wants and moods.

Whether you end up in a rambling, rickety house with half a dozen kids and cats, dogs and chickens or a chic penthouse suite with just the two of you, it really is your love that will keep you warm at nights, along with an incredible sense of belonging and strong family values.

So let's keep this simple and create a list of options that you can add to your master plan at the back of the book so you can identify him when you meet him. Your love match could be:

- A real estate agent
- A baker

- A fisherman
- A fishmonger
- A single dad
- A builder
- A cookery book writer
- A swimming instructor
- A man who owns a family business
- A genealogist
- A children's entertainer
- A health food store owner
- An historian
- A yachtsman
- A lifeguard

This list is by no means exhaustive and you can, and should, add some options of your own. You should be getting the picture by now. Think of the things you adore that include any form of being at home, cooking, family, history, being on or near water, and that's the kind of lover you should be drawing towards you, or putting yourself in a position to get closer to.

Which House is Your Venus in Cancer Sign In?

The astrological house that your Venus sign is in tells you even more about your ideal love match. If you haven't done it already, look back at the 'Find your Venus Sign' chapter for a quick and easy way to work it out.

First house: There's a softness to his skin, no matter what age he is, that makes him look younger than his years. He appears to be kind and indeed he is. His eyes seem to look into your heart and see your troubles and there's something about him that you feel is just plain huggable. He's vulnerable and sensitive, so treat him as you would wish to be treated.

Second house: This man is generous, almost to a fault. If he cares about you or about any particular cause or charity he's quite likely to give his money away in a swell of genuine emotion. That said, he also has a strong instinct for looking after his own creature comforts and those of his family, so is likely to be a hard worker and shrewd saver as well.

Third house: He'll be able to write an exquisite love letter and will never forget a birthday or an anniversary so cards and presents will arrive on time, every time. He'll expect you to do the same though and will be mortally offended if you forget or your gifts and cards to him are delayed. He'll love to try new restaurants and prefer those that have a homely feel to them and are in the neighborhood rather than miles away. He's also a one-man taxi service for you, your friends and family if needed. He might have a second home or mobile home or trailer by the sea.

Fourth house: This man is a great cook and prefers nothing more than preparing a sumptuous meal for friends, family and you. Prepare to be well fed, especially with aphrodisiac delights like oysters. Food is more than just a meal to him, it's a source of seduction and his reason for being alive. He's a real homebody too, so expect wherever he lives to be full of pictures of family and clutter from his childhood. He rarely gets rid of photos of old girlfriends either and may still be in touch with some of them. He doesn't mean anything by it, but beware if you're the jealous type.

Fifth house: He's great with kids and would probably love a houseful to look after, teach, nurture and play games with. He's also playfully romantic and will surprise you with gifts like plush toys and chocolates, and a trip to the park so he can push you on a swing. He's quite a flirt too, but he'll always make sure your needs are met, whether you're hungry, thirsty or in need of some TLC.

Sixth house: He'll know all about nutrition, and may even be a professional nutritionist as he loves food, but more than that he loves how good eating healthily makes him feel. He'll look after his body, and will be quite fussy about kitchen hygiene and tidiness around the home in general. It's possible that he keeps tropical fish.

Seventh house: This man is the great provider. His role in life is to look after his partner as she (and that could mean you) is the center of his universe. He'll always look out for you and protect you, which could feel a little smothering but the chances are you'll actually rather like that approach. He'll feel it's his responsibility to be the breadwinner but he'll expect to be looked after in a traditional sense, in that you'll need to keep house and cook, look after the children and be there whenever he needs you emotionally or otherwise. Or it may be the complete opposite and he'll be happy to be a house-husband while you go out to work.

Eighth house: He feels nurtured and nurturing through sex and money. You may not think it to look at him but this is what drives him. It's where he finds emotional fulfillment and he's going to make sure you're well looked after in this department too. Despite his sexy demeanor he's easily hurt, and he won't forgive or forget in a hurry. Food is a sensual pleasure for this guy and is a sure way to his heart and into his bed.

Ninth house: This man feels at home anywhere he goes, and the world is his university. He may travel with a favorite pillow or even a pair of slippers that remind him of home comforts, and he loves to learn about other cultures. He may be from a different country and he adores trying out foreign culinary delights. Adventurous and endlessly curious, he'll enjoy exploring new regions by recreational vehicle, taking his family with him.

Tenth house: He's likely to be the head of a family business. At worst, think *The Godfather* or *The Sopranos*, the kind of setup where you never take sides against the family, but more likely it's simply everyone pitching in to help and share, and make things better for the next generation who'll be taking care of business. He wants to build a dynasty, so having children and keeping the family name going are very important to him. He's a natural at making money as well as saving it for a rainy day.

Eleventh house: Friends are his extended family. He may still be living with them rather than on his own, or you may find that his pals use his place almost as their second home because it's such a warm and friendly environment to hang out in. You'll be expected to be part of that community and help out with feeding whoever happens to be around. He'll be your lover and your best friend though, and share your dreams, so that's pretty special.

Twelfth house: He's a bit of a worrier but he keeps it well hidden and may need some coaxing to reveal his true feelings as he's rather cautious about getting his heart broken. He'll admire you from a distance before having the nerve to make a move and it will be a subtle and sideways move at that, when it finally happens. He'll listen to all your woes with patience and will adore the fact that you've confided in him. More intuitive than most, he'll know how you're feeling and just what to say to make you feel better. Highly sensitive, be careful not to tread on his dreams.

Chapter 18

Who to Love if You Have Venus in Leo

When you have Venus in Leo, it's an almost foregone conclusion that you're in love with love. You adore the romance, the thrill of the chase, the flirtation, the dressing up to go out, the 'will he or won't he call' moments. All of it adds to a sense of drama and passion that puts the fun and playfulness into your romantic life.

If you're being completely honest with yourself though, do you find that once the honeymoon period is over, usually after the first six months of getting to know someone, things start to fizzle out and you have a hankering to move on and get that high of meeting someone new all over again? If so, your mission, should you choose to accept it, is to turn that initial romantic, flirtatious phase into something much longer lasting.

Truth be told, there may be an element of fear for you connected to committing to just one person. After all, how do you know if he or she is 'The One'? Part of finding love is about taking a gamble and if there's one thing you should surely be good at with Venus in Leo it's knowing when to take a risk, albeit a calculated one. And if you really put your mind to it you can be pretty lucky in the lottery of love.

So who are you looking for? He's cute, he's charming, endlessly entertaining and usually good with children. You may get the impression at times that he's still a big kid himself and he doesn't take kindly to having his fun curtailed in any way. He's a born romantic and will surprise you with flowers, jewelry and treats, and perhaps he'll even serenade you as he loves dramatic gestures that show him in a good light and make you blush with delight at sharing his shining moment.

He likes to be worshipped and the best way to get him to do anything is to flatter his ego, especially if it's doing something he really doesn't care for. You can persuade him to clean the bathroom or do the dishes and love it, if you approach him in the right way.

You're part of his ego boost so he'll want you to look good on his arm at all times, and accompany him to places to see and be seen. Whether it's to the local bar or to a first night opening at the theater, you looking the part will fill him with pride.

He will flirt but he'll always come back to you, as it's just a rather annoying, confidence-boosting game he feels he needs to play. The way to keep him and you happy and together is to plan regular date nights so that love never feels stale, routine or dull. And in the bedroom, dressing up and role playing will keep things fresh too.

You'll find him wherever he can find an audience. Holding court round the water cooler at work, telling flamboyant tales in the bar, at the racetrack making money or at the stock market, also making money.

He's a showman and possibly a musician so he'll be at home on the stage or simply entertaining friends at a party. He's a lot of fun but he can also be a lot of hard work.

One thing is you'll never be bored with him around and he'll also be great with kids if you have them. Added to that he's often exceedingly generous and will always make you feel a little bit special.

He also knows when to play the clown but has the respect of his peers as he knows how to lead and how to be industrious but how to make work fun too.

So let's keep this simple and create a list of options that you can add to your master plan at the back of the book so you can identify him when you meet him. Your love match could be:

- An actor
- A model
- A stockbroker

- A singer or musician
- A playboy
- A children's entertainer
- A racy novelist
- An entrepreneur
- A jeweler
- A party or events planner
- A casino croupier
- A director of films or plays
- A restaurant owner
- A hairdresser
- A creative team leader

This list is by no means exhaustive and you can, and should, add some options of your own. You should be getting the picture by now. Think of the things you adore that include any form of drama, passion, risk-taking, playfulness, flirtation, partying, flamboyance and creativity and that's the kind of lover you should be drawing towards you, or putting yourself in a position to get closer to.

Which House is Your Venus in Leo Sign In?

The astrological house that your Venus sign is in tells you even more about your ideal love match. If you haven't done it already, look back at the 'Find your Venus Sign' chapter for a quick and easy way to work it out.

First house: He is completely charismatic. His eyes scan the room and take in everything, making sure that all other eyes are on him. He's irresistible with a playfulness about him that's annoyingly attractive and he's supremely confident with no doubt whatsoever that he can win you over despite any resistance you may show. He might wear a distinctive piece of gold jewelry and may have great hair. He lives to be loved, and charm gets him through every situation.

Second house: You'll know him by his well-cut clothes and expensive watch. He loves the good things in life and goes the extra mile to make sure he can afford them. Opulent displays of wealth are his style but usually they'll be classy rather than tacky, though the occasional bit of 'bling' might slip through the net. Once smitten with you he'll be happy to extend his generosity to make sure you look as good as he does, though chances are you do already and that will be part of the mutual attraction.

Third house: He has great pick up lines. They may be corny but he delivers them with panache and makes them irresistible with a smile, and possibly a voice, to die for. He'll like to send sexy, flirty SMS messages or love poetry, and may write for a living. Sports, restaurants, theater and film reviews are his thing, or he'll simply love reading them and will be well informed and entertaining with hot news, sound advice and scandalous gossip.

Fourth house: His home is his castle and he's very much the ruler of his kingdom. Expect elements of drama and opulence in decor, especially in the bedroom, plus lots of photos of him, especially with trophies and awards he's won. He'll love to cook for you and prepare aphrodisiac feasts. What he really wants is a family of his own to worship him and to be proud of.

Fifth house: This one knows how to have fun. He's a dancer, a lover, a tease, a gambler with a lucky streak and he lives for pleasure and romance. He'll never lose that sense of first date excitement, and is in touch with his inner child. He's also very creative, either musically or theatrically, and that's how he may make a living. He's also marvelous with children as he instinctively knows what makes them tick.

Sixth house: Looking good is part of his game plan to attract success, both in business and with romance. He considers it an investment in himself and while he'll eat well and exercise he won't be averse to the odd bit of fake tan or a cosmetic procedure to enhance his already good looks. He's vain but he's gorgeous.

He may own a health club or be a personal trainer or hairdresser so he has to look the part.

Seventh house: He's an Alpha male, and no matter how evolved he says he is he still wants you to look good, make him look good and be seen as an A-list couple, whether you're out on the town together or just shopping for groceries. He wants to adore you and be adored. Money is no object when it comes to winning you, wining and dining you, then wedding you.

Eighth house: This one exudes power and wealth. He may be a little cagey about how he earns his money as he's a bit of an entrepreneur and wheeler-dealer but somehow it all comes good in the end. Sex is extremely important to him as it boosts his sense of power. He's a pussycat on the outside but a saber-toothed tiger within. He's very sensual, has a scent of wealth about him and shows it off in a dark and subtle way. He's more black Mercedes rather than red Ferrari.

Ninth house: Traveling in style is what he does best. Even if he's backpacking through Europe he'll have a cool rucksack and designer shades. He loves meeting new people and experiencing new cultures, especially their food and dance styles. He could be writing a travel guide about Ibiza or learning a new and deeper philosophy of life, but he'll make it fun and entertaining while he's doing it. He may also have major media potential, as there's a little bit of stardust about him. Don't be surprised if he's on TV, radio or in the movies.

Tenth house: He's top dog of whatever business he runs or owns. He's a great figurehead with massive charm and staying power to push his chosen industry up the ladder and into profit. Working hard is one thing but he understands the benefits of playing hard too so may throw lavish industry parties or treat his staff exceedingly well as an incentive for them to produce more and to be loyal, which for him is almost more important. He'll expect you to be at his side, mucking in with work and looking glamorous, ideally both at the same time.

Eleventh house: With him, friends aren't just friends. They're his support crew and fan club, cheering on whatever he does, so you're going to have to become one of them first and then fit in with them as he likes to travel with an entourage. He makes things happen, and the word 'impossible' is two letters too long for his liking. He's so confident but also so well connected that he seems to achieve miracles on a regular basis.

Twelfth house: It's all behind the scenes with him. He's generous, fun and entertaining but it's all quite low key. He'd rather have a one-on-one with you than be a party animal, but may play on your emotions to get the reaction he wants. He may even be able to turn on the tears at will to win your heart, especially if he thinks you're about to dump him. Potentially highly creative, he might be a gifted actor or an art therapist.

Chapter 19

Who to Love if You Have Venus in Virgo

Desperately seeking the perfect embodiment of love, your high hopes and higher standards can often leave you disappointed when it comes to romance when you have Venus in Virgo.

So what's the plan? You've taken the reins by reading this book and are doing what you usually do, which is to research the most efficient way to get what you want. But are you aware of what you actually need? The two things may be very different.

Setting standards is great. When it comes to dating it means you rarely drop below a level of personal comfort, and go out with men who are presentable, smart, easy on the eye and have something to say for themselves. But are you setting standards that are impossible to reach?

If life were to imitate art, yours might resemble the story, musical and film of *Guys and Dolls*. Take some time to check it out, since you're doing some research! The tale tells of neat, tidy Salvation Army gal Miss Sarah Brown who has her heart set on a particular type of man. 'I'll Know When My Love Comes Along', she sings in raptures about a solid, respectable man she has a firm picture of in her mind, from his sensible clothes to his dependable ways. Meanwhile cute, sexy and unpredictable gambler Sky Masterson reckons he'll leave love to chemistry and chance. Guess who she ends up with?

Similarly, it may be wise for you to be flexible about at least some of the rules you've mapped out for your Mr. Right and let nature (chemistry) and the stars (chance), steer you in the right direction.

By stepping out of your comfort zone you'll open yourself up to a world of new experiences that may have been closed off to you before. Yes, you know what you like and you like what you know, but if you haven't tried dating a different kind of guy then, like avoiding a different kind of food, how will you know whether it's to your taste?

The man you'll eventually end up with, sooner rather than later now that you've taken matters into your own hands, will already embody some of the things you're passionate about.

He may be good with animals, but work at an animal sanctuary rather than as a veterinarian. He could be a musician but play reggae rather than Rachmaninov. He could be involved in the world of publishing except that he's running a second-hand bookstore rather than writing an epic novel. And instead of being a squeaky clean, white-coated health specialist he could be a messy art therapist in paint-spattered overalls, a potter up to his elbows in sensual clay or an earthy gardener with mud on his boots.

And if he does turn out to be untidy and disorganized, who better than you to get him sorted out, spruced up and well-fed? Not that he's there to be changed, otherwise what's the point of being with him in the first place. A man doesn't come into your life finished and ready but then you're a work in progress too.

Which might be part of the problem. Secretly you may feel you're unlovable and may project your own perceived inadequacies onto someone potentially wonderful, even pointing out his supposed failings to his face, something you may not be aware that you do.

True love is about loving someone because of their flaws, not despite them, and a perfect relationship is not necessarily about having the perfect partner but doing things that bring an element of what feels like perfection and bliss into your life.

So kick your usual routine and embrace going with the flow. More than that, learn to embrace and love yourself just the way you are too. That's when you'll find love.

Get in touch with your hidden pleasure zones and rather than letting your inner critic dismiss either yourself or a potential partner as not good enough, you'll resonate openness, warmth and vitality which is way more alluring.

So let's keep this simple and create a list of options that you can add to your masterplan at the back of the book. Your love match could be:

- A veterinary surgeon
- A craftsman
- A nutritionist
- A bookseller
- A garden designer
- A personal trainer
- An art teacher
- A tailor
- A waiter
- A health store owner
- A massage therapist
- A librarian
- An accountant
- A dog walker
- A yoga teacher

This list is by no means exhaustive and you can, and should, add some options of your own. You should be getting the picture by now. Think of the things you adore that include any form of craft, organizing, serving or helping others, health, herbs or gardening, pets, and learning or gathering information and that's the kind of lover you should be drawing towards you, or putting yourself in a position to get closer to.

Which House is Your Venus in Virgo Sign In?

The astrological house that your Venus sign is in tells you even more about your ideal love match. If you haven't done it already, look back at the 'Find your Venus Sign' chapter for a quick and easy way to work it out.

First house: He's neat in very way. Even when he's casual he looks like he's stepped out of a catalogue. Fashionable though sometimes with a quirky take on style, he often wears glasses as he loves to read and pore over the internet so has worn out his eyes. He responds to equally well-groomed women, and if you smell natural and fresh like flowers or summer rain you'll appeal to his earthy senses.

Second house: This man is meticulous with money. He can account for every penny and feels uncomfortable if his figures don't tally, which is rare to the point of being unthinkable. He could be an accountant, a bank manager or a stock controller. He knows how to make money too and will research the best deals to invest in. He might be prudent with his cash and isn't averse to haggling for a bargain, though not in an unseemly manner. He'll just present his case with such logic that he can't help but get what he wants. When he finds a brand he likes he tends to stick with it.

Third house: You'll find him with his head in a book or surfing the net. He's an information junkie and loves to be kept informed about what's going on, especially in his neighborhood. Not that he's a gossip but he cares about the local environment and likes to have his finger on the community pulse. He could be a local newspaper reporter, or work in a local bookshop, health store or delicatessen. His speech and writing are very precise and he rarely chatters for the sake of it, wanting every conversation to be a useful exchange of ideas. He might also be a traveling salesman or use his car for work, so it doubles as an office.

Fourth house: His home is important to him, but while he's generally tidy it may not be a stylish place. For him home is functional, somewhere to eat and sleep and to store his books and clothes. He just might have a lush garden but it will be practical with herbs and vegetables, rather than be beautiful for the sake of it. The same goes for his kitchen where everything is designed for efficiency and health. He likes to use his hands so may bake his own bread, and he may make lots of home improvements which will be meticulously carried out.

Fifth house: Extraordinarily creative, he can usually turn his hand to anything from painting to gardening to making pots. His take on creativity is that it has to be practical and if it happens to be beautiful as well that's just a lucky bonus. He certainly appreciates beauty but favors function over form. When it comes to romance it's a different story. He has an eye for beautiful, near perfect women and even if he's with you and they're unattainable he won't be able to stop himself scrutinizing their every detail. He's also not above telling you your own flaws. Simply redirect him towards the mirror for a good look at himself if that occurs. When it comes to raising children, he'll be a firm but fair father, adept at teaching his family practical life skills.

Sixth house: There may be a slight obsession with keeping fit and staying young and attractive with this man. He values health and may push himself (and possibly you too) to the limit when it comes to endurance and getting the best out of the body. He can be a bit of a hypochondriac at times, but that said, he usually looks younger than his years and may be rather gorgeous to have around. He could work in the health industry as a nutritionist, or he may be involved with the care of domestic animals. He's good with his hands and very practical so may be a masseur, sports therapist or someone who makes useful items for a living. Gardening is another possible skill.

Seventh house: He's a perfectionist when it comes to whoever he has on his arm, so in his eyes you're highly favored if he wants you to be his partner. Although he can be quite fussy about having things a certain way, if you show him who's boss early on in the relationship he will concede to your authority. He's a great organizer who'll get things done superbly if you give him a to-do list so he can work his way through it. He doesn't think anyone can do things as well as he can, so tends to get on with it himself, not without the odd grumble or complaint as he can be a bit of a martyr, but everything will be accomplished to perfection.

Eighth house: When it comes to the bedroom, this guy is curious and inventive. Though he may be quite powerful in his career he's intrigued by the idea of being dominated so expect some bedroom role-play to spice things up. He's clever with money, often making sound investments for other people as well as for himself. A little on the cautious side about his well-being, he gets good deals on life and health insurance. He may be a financial researcher, a sex therapist, or a tax inspector. He's intuitive and rather suspicious so there's no point trying to hide anything from him.

Ninth house: This man is a walking encyclopedia. He has knowledge at his fingertips and loves to share it. He may be a teacher specializing in art and crafts, a botanist or someone who travels to other countries to promote health care. Learning and education are extremely important to him, and he loves to debate life's bigger issues. Unusual philosophies appeal to him, but only if he can find a logic to them, as he's open and fascinated but far from gullible. He likes to be prepared for emergencies when traveling so packs light but often carries a range of medicinal products just in case, as he's extremely organized and pragmatic. He could be a writer of non-fiction 'how to' books or a compiler of dictionaries.

Tenth house: Even if he runs his own company, he tends to get involved with everything. Partly it's because he doesn't trust anyone to get things right and also because it feels more natural to him to be of service to others. He's terribly critical, it has to be said, and won't waste words on softening the verbal blow if there's anything that fails to satisfy. He tells it like it is, or at least how he sees it, although when it comes to health care and benefits he does look after his staff. He could be involved with an ecological, ethical business, or be responsible for drawing up watertight contracts. He'll stay in the same job forever, once he's found his niche. Money and status are important to him, but only for the stability they bring him and his loved ones.

Eleventh house: His friends are like a brotherhood to him. He's either known them since school or has formed a bond through work or some sort of organization he belongs to. Together they may be involved in helping others or are united by something they like to do, like a guild of craftsmen. If he introduces you to his friends you're 'in'. He's very particular about who he socializes with so sharing similar interests and values is more important to him than for most others. He may not have a huge number of friends as a result, but he loves to arrange and organize things for them so is a bit of a social mover and shaker.

Twelfth house: He may seem rather aloof at first. It's partly shyness but also he's quite hard on himself and self-critical so he often doesn't feel he's good enough to make the first move. At the same time, he can come across as being quite critical of others, but it's a self-defense mechanism to protect his own self-esteem. He gets things done behind the scenes and often doesn't want or seek thanks or praise. He'll also do anything to help you, as he sees himself as a knight in shining armor. He may not be the most romantic of men but he'll show his love by making things, fixing things and giving you a hug and a hot drink (or glass of wine) just when you need it.

Chapter 20

Who to Love if You Have Venus in Libra

Tasteful, elegant, refined, slow to anger, quick to praise, this is the vision of loveliness that embodies the person who has Venus in Libra.

So that's mainly you, but it also shows very clearly the kind of man who would complement you. Venus is the planet that rules Libra so it's an extra special combination. It's the planet of love in the sign of relationships so finding your other half is a personal quest of yours, and most likely has been for more years than you care to remember.

Loving and sharing make your world go around and the chances are that you feel somehow incomplete without a partner at your side. Yet often you're so eager to please and be the peacemaker that you go along with things and stay in relationships that really aren't suitable for you, partly to have that feeling of belonging and completeness but also because you're fair minded and hate to offend anyone who's been decent enough to declare an interest in you.

That has to stop. It's your life and you need to live it to your own high standards, not just be a people pleaser for the sake of peace.

So who do you want and where do you find him? Venus in Libra draws you to lovers who are undoubtedly attractive, but not necessarily in the conventional sense. They have to look good in your eyes, but it's also partly to do with them resonating a feeling of calm and harmony that matches your own, as much as looking the part.

Your ideal man must appreciate some of the finer things in life and be a creative thinker. Architecture, photography and art may be areas he's interested in, rather good at as a pastime or even earns an income from. He likes to think before he speaks, and is fair-minded and eloquent. He could be a lawyer or a counselor, and can see both sides of an argument, which makes him a force to be reckoned with professionally but on a personal level can be frustrating as he can come across as indecisive.

You could meet him at an art gallery, on the stage, making a presentation, or at a fashion show as he's a snappy dresser. At a party he'll be the one handing out drinks and nibbles to make sure everyone has their fair share and feels comfortable and at ease.

Loud, brash behavior is a real turn off for him and subtlety, good manners and witty conversation are what he does best, and what he likes best in his soulmate. He may seem a little detached at first but once he's smitten he'll be at your side forever more.

He's the ultimate romantic so expect to dress up, share candlelit dinners, dance close, receive flowers, take handheld walks through the city rather than the countryside, and indulge in weekends away in stylish hotels.

In bed he makes love in every sense. It's a completely sensual experience with this guy, never a hurried fumble in the dark as he's way too classy for that. Expect an earth shattering joining of minds, bodies and souls.

Look for him wherever you already do things that you love. He could be your hairdresser as he adores creating or enhancing beauty, or he could run or work at your favorite spa.

Check out places where justice is seen to be done, at the courts or where human rights are important issues, and discussion groups, book clubs and philosophy courses are potential hangouts too.

You could meet him at an organized dating event as he truly needs a partner in his life to feel whole. Or he may catch your eye at a work-related social gathering where he'll genuinely be interested in what you do as he's great at small talk but he actually listens and makes a mental note of what's been said.

So let's keep this simple and create a list of options that you can add to your master plan at the back of the book so you can identify him when you meet him. Your love match could be:

- A lawyer
- A counselor
- A hairdresser
- A diplomat
- A judge
- A fashion designer
- A spa manager
- A charity fundraiser
- An HR manager
- A designer goods store owner
- A gallery owner
- An architect
- A style advisor
- A jewelry maker or jewelry store owner
- An actor

This list is by no means exhaustive and you can, and should, add some options of your own. You should be getting the picture by now. Think of the things you adore that include any form of beauty, harmony, debate, art, fashion and fair dealing and that's the kind of lover you should be drawing towards you, or putting yourself in a position to get closer to.

Which House is Your Venus in Libra Sign In?

The astrological house that your Venus sign is in tells you even more about your ideal love match. If you haven't done it already, look back at the 'Find your Venus Sign' chapter for a quick and easy way to work it out.

First house: He's drop dead gorgeous, a little aloof and well dressed so even if his jeans are ripped you can be sure he's paid a lot for that look. He exudes understated charm and may seem a little in touch with his feminine side, almost pretty rather than handsome, which somehow just makes him more attractive. He might be an actor or a model, or work in PR. He has a knack of being whatever you want him be so it may take a while to get to know the real him.

Second house: This man is a money magnet, but again it's understated not brash, flash or in your face bling. He likes to share his wealth, and will be quick to pay for dinner or drinks, and he most likely gives money to charitable causes connected to art or architecture. He's tactile and you'll want to touch him as his clothes will be soft and sensual and he'll smell heavenly.

Third house: Words of love come really easily to this guy. He manages to make the simplest sentiments sound fresh and heartfelt, and coming from him and his dulcet-toned voice, indeed they are. He can charm the birds out of the trees, you into bed and tightwads to part with their money for charity. He writes beautifully too.

Fourth house: This man loves his home. It's likely to be full of gadgets and be sleek, minimal and modern with lots of pale colors and white walls. He also loves to cook and may be a dab hand at desserts, having something of a sweet tooth. He's a people person so home is where he's happiest to have friends to talk, laugh, share ideas and relax with. More to the point, you'll feel at home with him too.

Fifth house: He's a love magnet, but in a gentle, refined way. Something about him oozes charm and he can win anyone over, seemingly without even making an effort. He's a target for women, with his delightful manners, light touch and soft voice, so be proud of him rather than possessive if you can. He's also good with children but would expect them to be immaculate, never grubby. He'll be great at encouraging their creativity through fun things to do. He's into romance and will win you over with all the usual trimmings but definitely in a non-cheesy way. Prepare to swoon!

Sixth house: This guy is fit. He knows how to look good, what to eat and may even be a little narcissistic. But he'll be so easy on the eye it will be worth letting him hog the mirror more than you do. Work-wise, he gets organized by filing things in aesthetically pleasing ways with designer folders on retro desks, that's when he's not glued to the sleekest available cell phone or laptop. Anything that pares things down enough to be stylish and functional suits this equally aesthetically pleasing guy. He's a bit of a neat freak, perhaps a touch OCD, but chances are you're quite similar so it could be a match made in heaven.

Seventh house: He's the man every other woman would like to have on her arm or in her home (or bed). He looks good, he has perfect manners, he lets you make all the important decisions and, more than that, he loves you to bits. He feels complete in a relationship and will do his darnedest to make sure things are harmonious as fights and rows deplete him more than they would most other people. That said, once riled he'll explode like a firework, so stand well back!

Eighth house: Money and passion are the keys to this man. He has a knack of making money and he does it as well as, if not better than, the way he makes love. He has a subtle power in the boardroom and in the bedroom, and he can make people do things they didn't mean to do, whether that's parting with cash to invest in his business or seducing you when you had every intention of going home. Either scenario will be so beautifully done that you won't object at all and will keep coming back for more. He has an air of elegant mystery that's irresistible.

Ninth house: Your first impression of this guy is that he's well-read, well-informed and thoroughly fascinating. He knows (probably) more than you do, but won't make you feel inferior or ignorant as a result. In fact every encounter with him will be enlightening, so much so that you probably didn't realize that learning could be so much fun. He might be a tutor or lecturer, a researcher or PR person whose charm helps him represent places and people who aren't so skilled in diplomacy and elegance as he is.

Tenth house: His career is super-important to him and he's the kind of man to build up an empire, potentially in an area that focuses on beauty. He might run a salon or spa, be a motivational speaker or counselor or a therapist. He dresses for success, with smart clothes and understated signs of wealth. He doesn't do flashy, but those in the know will recognize the statement watch or designer shirt. He'll surround himself with attractive staff and if family are involved in his enterprises he'll want them to look good and make him proud.

Eleventh house: This guy is a wonderful friend. He'll want to be your friend way before he becomes your lover as that, to him, is a sure sign of staying power in a romantic relationship. He's generous to his pals and adds an air of laid-back, slightly air-heady cool to any gathering. He'll be the one strumming a guitar absent-mindedly at a summer's day picnic. He has a way of making his hopes and dreams come true almost effortlessly too, as people just seem to be there to help him along the way.

Twelfth house: He's a bit of a dark horse, in that he won't declare his feelings of love for fear of rejection. He may admire you from afar for a long time before making a move. He's the strong, silent type, wanting to sweep you off your feet one moment but almost needing you to do the same for him the next. And he does seem able to get people to look after him with his kind of cute but helpless persona. He might be hard work at times but you'll think he's worth it.

Chapter 21

Who to Love if You Have Venus in Scorpio

Venus the planet of love in Scorpio the sign of sex? You're in real trouble!

In fact it's a beautiful thing, because while it's true that with Venus in Scorpio sexuality is heightened, so is the depth of feeling, so when you bond with someone you truly intend to bond for life.

That may be part of the problem because this combination also has a tendency to make you rather possessive, which can lead to jealousy and suspicion. And, should things go wrong and you do part company, it's very hard for you to let go of someone who's been close enough to share some of your darkest secrets and most private thoughts.

If you're not careful, you can end up bringing your past relationships into your present relationships, and in the process mess up a promising future with someone wonderful. Who wants to be reminded of your exes when they're in a relationship with you? Put the boot on the other foot and you'd go wild if someone you were dating brought up his last partner's name at an inappropriate moment.

One way around this is to do the other thing that's very Scorpionic, and that's to detox, declutter and effectively decontaminate your heart, mind and soul of painful reminders.

That's not to say you should totally obliterate the memory of someone you cared about by ripping up photos and burning old love letters, although therapeutically and karmically for you and for your new Significant Other that's not such a bad idea. But storing them away in a nook of your memory that's only activated by hearing a certain song, a hint of a particular scent or aftershave, or passing by a café or restaurant where you shared good times is perfectly acceptable.

How bad can it get? A photographer client of mine had a Venus in Scorpio partner who insisted that an arty photo on the wall featuring a blurred image of his ex had to be removed. That's fair enough, but after she too had faded from his life he realized that she'd been through his old photo albums and removed all the pictures of the offending ex, and had even cut her face out of any photos featuring him.

With Venus in Scorpio there are times when you may be on the verge of committing a similar crazy crime of passion. So, putting intense, obsessive behavior aside, what should you be looking for in a partner?

In some ways you do want someone as intense as yourself as, if you're honest, you rather like and (some might say) thrive on the potential drama that goes with a relationship. You want someone who can make you melt with his gaze, come alive with his touch, infuriate you with his mysterious ways but who truly understands that the whole point of a row is to make up again, ideally horizontally.

Love means way more to you than having a passive 'yes' man who just falls asleep in front of the TV every night.

With Venus in Scorpio you need to have your desires and senses stimulated by someone tactile, who breaks taboos, and who doesn't care who sees you in a full-on Public Display of Affection, kissing him passionately in the street.

There's a lot of sexual energy and tension between you and you'll probably wind each other up for the sheer hell of it. Others may not understand the intensity of your connection and may even think you're being ridiculously kind then unbelievably cruel to each other, but you both know exactly what you're doing and understand the rules of the game and its limits.

Where to find him? Look to where you find pleasure in life already and that's where you could meet your love match.

If you love to read or even write steamy novels, he could be an author at a local bookstore signing or a fellow student at a creative writing class.

If you're canny with money he could be an equally clever financial advisor who knows how to reduce your tax bills or has mysterious but legal offshore investment funds to protect your hard-earned cash.

Always wanted to learn to tango? He's your ideal dance partner in every sense, full of passion and with some sultry moves that will sweep you off your feet.

He's the strong, silent type whose eyes and body language say more than words ever can. You'll never be bored with him though life may be a little tempestuous at times. So long as there's trust, respect and honesty between you, you'll open your hearts and your souls to each other like never before.

There's a real element of karma about a union where Venus in Scorpio is concerned, as if you'd met in another life and have unfinished business to attend to. Get it right this time around and you'll evolve to be a more complete being with a wonderful relationship that will make you feel like you've finally achieved nirvana.

So let's keep this simple and create a list of options that you can add to your master plan at the back of the book so you can identify him when you meet him. Your love match could be:

- A banker
- A researcher
- A crime writer
- An astrologer
- A sex therapist
- A psychic
- An entrepreneur
- A detox therapist
- A psychiatrist
- A spy

- A private detective
- An exotic dancer
- A hypnotherapist
- A miner
- A plumber

This list is by no means exhaustive and you can, and should, add some options of your own. You should be getting the picture by now. Think of the things you adore that include life's mysteries, sensual pleasures, things that are underneath the squeaky clean surface of life, people with incredible depth and insight, and that's the kind of lover you should be drawing towards you, or putting yourself in a position to get closer to.

Which House is Your Venus in Scorpio Sign In?

The astrological house that your Venus sign is in tells you even more about your ideal love match. If you haven't done it already, look back at the 'Find your Venus Sign' chapter for a quick and easy way to work it out.

First house: His eyes are mesmerizing. Once you have eye contact with him you won't be able to tear yourself away from his gaze that seems to look right into you and know your every secret. He has a dark and brooding, seriously sexy charisma. He could be a model or a therapist, and has an ability to draw people to him without even trying, so magnetic is his personality. He loves to wear black.

Second house: This guy has secret reserves of money. He may not say where it comes from, and it doesn't necessarily mean it's coming from underhand sources, but he may be tight-lipped about exactly how he earns his cash. It could be that he's a little embarrassed as it could be from recycling, waste disposal or drain clearing so not as sexy as the image he likes to portray. He likes to display his wealth in subtle and stylish ways.

Third house: The object of your desire loves to SMS, sext, and get under your skin with words and emails. He's a gold mine of information about all sorts of mysterious things and can find out anything about anything and anyone as his research skills are second to none. He could be a private detective or investigative journalist. Don't try to keep secrets from him as he's super-suspicious too.

Fourth house: He loves to analyze things to get to the very core of them. He may have family issues, perhaps conflicts about being a father, brother or son and a sensual individual alongside those roles. He may have a family secret or simply be extremely devoted to his family, including and especially the one he may hope to have with you. Home is a sensual playground for him, full of aphrodisiac food and tactile but masculine furnishings.

Fifth house: He's a tease and you both know it. He loves to flirt and does it in a very low key but sensual way. He'll love to dress to impress and stand out from the crowd, with well-cut and immaculate clothes, and he looks great in black. He's likely to be an excellent dancer and will be more than happy to show you some raunchy moves on the dance floor.

Sixth house: He looks after himself. He may not be a gym fanatic, preferring to work the magic at home rather than get hot and sweaty in a public display of 'my abs are better than yours' at the gym. He'll just make sure his are better than anyone else's in a subtle and sexy way. He doesn't go for an over-developed muscleman build, although he will work out intensively to achieve the aesthetic look he wants. He's also a mover and shaker behind the scenes at work, getting things done without necessarily seeking reward or appreciation for it, but knowing full well that the place would genuinely fall apart without him.

Seventh house: This man bonds for life. You're his and he's yours. End of story. He'll do all he can to keep you and to make you happy, financially, physically and emotionally. All he asks in return is unwavering loyalty, trust, honesty and faithfulness. That's a big ask, but you'll get exactly the same right back so what's not to love? You'll share your deepest dreams and darkest secrets together and will feel united against the world.

Eighth house: He's sexy (there's that word again) and powerful. Enigmatic too, so you won't ever know what's really going on in his mind, and it's probably better not to. He may be involved in secret business deals, not necessarily shady but things that are better left behind closed boardroom doors. He may be handsome-ugly, that odd alluring mix of pheromones and power that makes certain men strangely irresistible.

Ninth house: This man is unfathomably deep. He has knowledge at his fingertips and seems to understand life's mysteries, although he may also be one of life's mysteries himself. If he travels, it'll be to unknown territory. He could be a media guru or simply a guru as he's charismatic and sexually magnetic at the same time. He might be a broadcaster or writer of spiritual books, or just the sexiest teacher ever.

Tenth house: Powerful, a leader, the boss. No two ways about it, this man is in charge of whatever he does, and even if he appears to be a silent partner he's pulling the strings in the background. He's 'old school' money, though he may also have made some dubious investments to boost the coffers that he'd rather not mention. He's dark and brooding, and you can almost hear his business mind whirring. He might look distinguished and command respect, but he drips with understated sex appeal.

Eleventh house: If you're invited into his entourage, consider yourself honored. He may know lots of people but there are very few that he trusts enough to call his friends. Discussing life's deeper meanings, emotions and conspiracy theories may be among his favorite things to do. What's said amongst friends, stays amongst friends, as if you've joined a secret society or a group with a very particular code of honor.

Twelfth house: This man can see into your heart. At last it feels like he can. He'll hold your gaze and make you feel like you're the only person in the world worth spending time with.

Then he'll go and do the same with someone else! It's just his way, wanting whoever he's talking with to feel they have his undivided attention. That said, he'll do anything for you once he's truly smitten. He'll want to rescue you, save you, envelop you with love and affection, and will expect you to do the same for him. He's deeply intuitive and most likely knows what you're going to do and say before it happens. You'll complete not just each other's sentences, but will complete each other too.

Chapter 22

Who to Love if You Have Venus in Sagittarius

There's not enough love in the world. That's your philosophy of life and you go out of your way to remedy that sorry situation.

You tend to open your heart to most people, in the belief that they're innocent of crimes against love until proven guilty so why not take the chance? Venus in Sagittarius is very much about that kind of universal justice, but it's also about risk and adventure.

Your natural warmth and sense of humor are great for attracting men your way. You most probably like to and can talk to anyone, and are great at making them laugh too. The trouble is guys think you're coming on to them even if you're just being friendly, so you may find you get all sorts of unsuitable types wanting to get more than just friendly with you simply because you're being nice and they're misreading the signals.

You're not great at details, so there's a chance you may be misreading their signals too and not getting the fact that, in their minds, they've already passed the friendship stage and want something more.

Clearly you can't help the way nature made you, but being aware of the subtle messages your body's sending out could help you in the long run to avoid yet another ill-advised match with someone you know isn't really suitable but who you think may be worth taking a gamble on.

Here's a thought. With Venus in Sagittarius you love to learn new stuff, especially anything connected to broadening your outlook and understanding human nature a little better, so why not invest some time in studying how to read body language? You'd be brilliant at it as you pick things up quickly, and it would save you a lot of grief and trouble in the romance department.

Once you've mastered that, where are you going to find the man who 'gets' you as much as you 'get' him?

He loves to laugh as much as you do so a comedy club or comedy film night would be a good bet. You're also both adventurers at heart so you might meet him while traveling or even just on a walk in the great outdoors. Wherever you feel free and happy is where you'll look your best and will be sending out some very clear messages with those all important body language signals too.

He could be a teacher at a class you attend or at a school function for your own or someone else's child. He's a smart cookie, that's for sure, and you'll fall for his beautiful mind as much as for his haphazard mix of ruggedness and 'lost professor' look.

He could be a tour guide who's passionate about his subject so don't rule out taking a trip with an adventure travel company to meet the man of your dreams.

Look to the things you already love to help you find your soulmate too.

He could be in the media, on TV, or the author or a fan of your favorite life-changing self-help book.

He might be a comedian or someone who works with wild animals, so book yourself on a safari holiday or explore the local zoo to check out the keepers rather than the animals. You could even find him in your nearest museum of natural history as he's a bit of a boffin, and university towns are also perfect places for the kind of man you should become intellectually and emotionally intertwined with.

And as for his style, it won't be orthodox, that's for sure. He's a law unto himself, but may have a thing for loud Hawaiian shirts and t-shirts with comic slogans. He could wear bling jewelry or be a fan of bow ties. He may dress as if he just doesn't care and the truth is he really doesn't. He'd probably be happier naked if he knew he wouldn't get into trouble as he really relishes freedom, so may go 'commando' as a minor protest about restriction and protocol.

That said, he could be a champion of the underdog in the law courts. If so his signature delivery will be fair but funny whether he's a barrister or, potentially at some later stage in his life, a judge. He's a firm believer in justice for all.

He's also rather lucky and things do seem to fall into his lap. At its worst it could mean he has a liking for taking risks without weighing up the odds, but on the plus side whatever he does seems to work out in his favor in some way. Make sure he gets a lucky break by having you in his life.

So let's keep this simple and create a list of options that you can add to your master plan at the back of the book so you can identify him when you meet him. Your love match could be:

- A comedian
- A philosopher
- A gambler
- A tutor
- A freedom fighter
- An advertising salesperson
- A TV news reporter
- A professor
- A judge
- A travel guide
- A zookeeper
- A safari guide
- A spiritual teacher
- An opera singer
- A long distance truck driver

This list is by no means exhaustive and you can, and should, add some options of your own. You should be getting the picture by now. Think of the things you adore that include any form of media, comedy, education, spirituality or travel and anything that's done on a grand scale, and that's the kind of lover you should be drawing towards you, or putting yourself in a position to get closer to.

Which House is Your Venus in Sagittarius Sign In?

The astrological house that your Venus sign is in tells you even more about your ideal love match. If you haven't done it already, look back at the 'Find your Venus Sign' chapter for a quick and easy way to work it out.

First house: You'll recognize him by his broad smile, and possibly by his suntanned or slightly weather-beaten face as he loves the outdoors. He's a little bit vain so may even apply fake tan because it makes him feel he looks better. He's got a great laugh, loud but pleasing to the ear and infectious, and a generally happy take on life. Bright colors cheer him up so eye-popping t-shirts and patterned shirts make him stand out from the crowd.

Second house: This guy has a way with making money. He's fearless so will invest in things without knowing all the details and more often than not will get a good return on his investment. He has a lucky streak that only fails him occasionally but it can be quite a major event when it does. Somehow he always seems to bounce back from adversity and it never stops him from being generous, especially to those he loves.

Third house: He loves to learn and to teach, as well as to write and to talk. Endlessly fascinated and curious about everything, he might like to gossip or could be the top reporter for a national newspaper. Sometimes it may seem like he talks a little too much, but he can tell jokes and anecdotes, stories and tall tales that can hold an audience enthralled. He likes to be on the move too, so could be a cab driver with the double benefit (for him) of traveling but being able to converse with different people every day.

Fourth house: This man lives to cook and to eat. He may particularly enjoy foods from different countries and trying out new flavors and new recipes. Barbecues and eating outdoors in general, especially if camping with the family, are among his favorite exploits. He might be a little on the heavy side physically, but he'll be a good kisser as his mouth is extremely sensitive to new sensations and tastes. Food is like a meditation for him, whether preparing it or eating it. He might bake wittily shaped cakes or write cookbooks and he will certainly make a mess in the kitchen but the results will be worth it.

Fifth house: He's a bit of a risk-taker but his gambles generally pay off. He's hugely flirtatious and will laugh you into bed, as his sense of humor is both sexy and irresistible. He may have an extremely creative streak, and could produce art on a large scale. Colorful and bright landscapes and meditative spiritual pieces may be his strengths. He's also likely to be extremely good with children, and may want a whole soccer team's worth of his own one day.

Sixth house: When it comes to both fitness and work, outdoors is where you're likely to find your love match. He doesn't really do the gym, preferring to hike or run in the hills if possible. He may have an outdoorsy job, working with large animals, or something that keeps him very mobile schmoozing with clients around the country or traveling internationally. He's usually a picture of health but can be prone to overdoing things and forgetting to take care of himself.

Seventh house: Prepare to be charmed, loved, and made happier than you ever have been with this man. He puts his all into his relationships. He does things on a big scale so if you end up marrying him expect all the trimmings and a wedding day that has people talking about it for a long time afterwards. Love is an adventure for him and he wants you as his traveling companion through life. He, and you, will need some personal freedom to function fully though, so allow some breathing spaces in your togetherness, for both your sakes.

Eighth house: He's a wheeler-dealer with lots of secret deals on the go, many of which are extremely profitable. He may run a casino or back political parties, or simply have a shrewd head for business that may not be immediately obvious from his devil-may-care, laid-back attitude and his dark sense of humor. He gets a thrill from the power and passion of taking financial risks, and is likely to have a powerful libido too.

Ninth house: This man is in his element when he's traveling, teaching or learning. He may be very spiritual, perhaps a popular yoga teacher, but equally he could be someone in the public eye as some kind of guru, advisor or counselor. If he works in the field of law, he's extremely fair-minded and will go out of his way to see that justice is done. He's also a lot of fun to be with thanks to his eternally optimistic outlook on life.

Tenth house: He works hard but he turns it into play so that work is not only profitable but enjoyable too. As a boss, which he's more than likely to be, he's a great motivator and a pleasure to work for. And though he may be lacking in organizational skills he inspires the kind of loyalty that makes other people look after that kind of thing for him. Generous to staff, he also likes to treat himself and the ones he loves to the good things in life with the money he earns, believing wholeheartedly that life is to be enjoyed and not just endured.

Eleventh house: Friends are his complete and utter joy. He gets everything he needs from them so you may have a job on your hands finding 'alone time' with him as he prefers to be surrounded by groups of people who make him laugh and who he can entertain as chief joker. He makes friends wherever he goes as he has such an easygoing charm. He's the one others turn to for adventure and advice, as he's also wiser than he likes to appear. Giving him freedom within your relationship and becoming his best friend will make him all yours forever.

Twelfth house: He'll love you from afar before letting you know he's fallen for you. He's a very spiritual type and quite sensitive, possibly extremely intuitive as well so he may know what you're thinking before you do. He might be a therapist or counselor, or someone who trains others in those fields. He's happy to talk about feelings and has a knack of making other people feel optimistic and hopeful when they're low. He may be a fabulous artist or dancer but tends to keep these things hidden for fear of being made fun of, although he can take a joke and can be entertainingly self-deprecating.

Chapter 23

Who to Love if You Have Venus in Capricorn

If you have Venus in Capricorn you have tastes that are grounded in quality and longevity, and that applies to the men in your life too.

You can appreciate the history and the value of something that's made for endurance and to pass the test of time rather than just as a passing fad, and there's a strong chance that, given the choice, you'd opt for a partner who is older and wiser than yourself.

No matter how independent you are, there's something you find deeply attractive and reassuring about an older man. You might even start a relationship with someone senior in the company you work for as you rather like the sense of power that goes with such an alliance. Not that you're only after his money, although you more than most appreciate that age and wisdom also bring financial security and stability.

On the other hand, you may be attracted to men who are significantly younger than you, or find that you keep attracting types who are keen to benefit from your wisdom and who find both your sense of style and your power extremely alluring. There's something about you that exudes a subtle sexiness that appeals to a certain kind of man who appreciates everything an older woman has to offer. This could apply to you whether you're 26 or 46 so don't knock it!

If you haven't been attracted to either of these options in the past or have but not followed through, that could be where you've been going wrong in your search for love.

Because you're a stickler for convention, part of you may be resisting your natural inclinations as society even now thinks it's not exactly wrong but maybe a little unorthodox to have a larger than expected age gap in a relationship, especially if you're a woman dating a considerably younger man. But so what? You can't help who you're attracted to and suppressing your true nature for the sake of appearances is plain crazy. Live your truth.

Once you've got over that particular barrier, you can set your mind to working out who he might be and where to find him.

Regardless of age, he has leadership quality written all over him. He may be at the top of the company he works for, he owns it or is in a family business and being groomed to take over at some stage. He does things in a traditional way, with courtesy and manners, but it's not a good idea to cross him in business or in love as once he's made his mind up about something or someone he won't budge on changing it.

The man you're seeking has a reserved kind of charm and may even seem a little stilted or awkward at first. But he'll wear you down with his calm and persuasive persistence so that he gets under your skin and into your heart before you know it. He's by no means a smooth operator or fast worker, but he'll wine and dine you at some of the best places in town and not expect you to pay. He will see this as an investment in his and your future, however, so if he feels like he's being used as a meal ticket he'll be out the door and on his way without a backwards glance.

He likes to lay down solid foundations for anything he's involved with so he could be an architect or a builder, potentially connected with preserving historic buildings as well as the construction of new ones.

He's shrewd with money so you may find him ensconced in banking institutions. Adventurous Venus in Capricorn types often have a fascination with mountains and love to be out in the cool mountain air, so perhaps factor that into your next vacation destination or consider doing a sponsored mountain trek for charity and you might encounter him on the long climb up.

He's also fascinated by structure and this includes the human body too so he could be a chiropractor or orthopedic surgeon, or possibly be in need of one!

Creatively he's more attuned to art as an investment, and is likely to buy or create things that last, like sculptures or property.

Respect, tradition, mutual support and faithfulness are what this guy wants, as in fact do you if you're honest with yourself. It doesn't mean things can't be glitzy, romantic or fun at times too but when it's not he'll help you weather all sorts of storms with his pragmatic approach.

And if you want someone in your life for the rest of it, he's your man, because once he's smitten he's in it for the long haul.

So let's keep this simple and create a list of options that you can add to your master plan at the back of the book so you can identify him when you meet him. Your love match could be:

- A banker
- A construction worker
- An architect
- An osteopath
- A dentist
- A sculptor
- A curator
- A mountaineer
- A geologist
- A jeweler
- An antiques auctioneer
- A politician
- A renovator of old buildings
- A stonemason
- An historian

This list is by no means exhaustive and you can, and should, add some options of your own. You should be getting the picture by now. Think of the things you adore that include any form of heritage, tradition, respectability and longevity, power and authority and doing things the proper way not the quick fix way, and that's the kind of lover you should be drawing towards you, or putting yourself in a position to get closer to.

Which House is Your Venus in Capricorn Sign In?

The astrological house that your Venus sign is in tells you even more about your ideal love match. If you haven't done it already, look back at the 'Find your Venus Sign' chapter for a quick and easy way to work it out.

First house: He cuts quite a dash with his classic clothes made to last, and he always dresses perfectly for the occasion. He may have chiseled cheekbones, distinctive teeth and a very upright walk. He could be quite clipped in his manner but you can sense the warmth underneath, waiting to emerge once he gets to know and trust you. He can be a little formal at first but has an air of authority that is very attractive.

Second house: This one knows all about investments and money. He may come across as a little guarded with his cash at first but if he's going to invest in you as a partner he'll soon learn to open up his wallet. He adores quality and buys items that are timeless, not just this season's 'must haves'. There's a hint of 'old money' about him and he's likely to have shopped at the same places for years.

Third house: He doesn't say much but when he does he makes it count. He has a wonderfully dry sense of humor and can make people fall about laughing with just a word, as his sense of comic timing is spot on. He may send you handwritten love letters as he likes things to last, not to be lost in a flurry of easily deletable SMS messages and emails. He might like to read the classics and keeps up with the news through a traditional newspaper even though he may be reading it on his laptop. Education is something he values highly, and he could be a well-respected teacher.

Fourth house: This man loves food. It nurtures him and he prefers classic dishes and old family favorites, the kind of comfort food his mother used to make. He shops or potentially works at a traditional family-run butchers or bakers, and buys edible treats in fine food halls when he can. He can't bear eating to excess and prefers quality to quantity. He's also a stickler for family values and expects his partner and children to present a united and dignified front to the world, and to make him proud at all times.

Fifth house: He has a creative streak and likes to produce things that stand the test of time. If he isn't a sculptor himself this may be his favorite art form. He might collect rocks or fossils, or deal in gemstones. He's excellent if sometimes a little strict with children, wanting to give them a solid foundation in life. He can be a little shy or rather formal when it comes to romance, though. It's all about pacing himself, and he hates to be rushed so if things seem stilted at first have patience and his affectionate side will show through.

Sixth house: Being fit and healthy is second nature to this guy, and he'll invest in good health care schemes and insurance to make sure he gets the best advice and treatment available. Prevention is better than cure in his eyes as he wants to live forever if he possibly can. He might eat a restricted diet and be on the thin side but he'll look good on it and appear younger than his years. He's quite fussy about being organized and punctual and would expect you to take care of your health and always be on time too.

Seventh house: He's an asset to you as you are an asset to him. Pillars of the community together, he'd want you to help him achieve 'The Couple Everyone Else Wants To Be' status. Very traditional in his outlook, he'd most likely want you to stay at home and look after the kids, but he'll be happy to have you help him run his business, and respectful and proud if you've carved out a position of authority or business of your own.

Eighth house: Mystery is the name of his game. Not that he's trying to deceive you but he's a very private person who doesn't like to divulge his secrets until he trusts you absolutely. There's a sense of power and authority about him, and he may like to indulge in role playing games in the bedroom. He appears to have plenty of money but is never ostentatious with it.

Ninth house: He has firm beliefs about the world, and they give him comfort. He might be quite conservative in his outlook, but he is a spiritual person. Higher education is highly important to him and knowledge is his currency in life. He may be the head of a college or university, a teacher of history, politics, math or business studies, and his word is the law! He's also possibly involved with the legal profession career-wise. He's fiercely intelligent but might be a little prudish at times.

Tenth house: A smart businessman, he's likely to be building an empire if not a dynasty that he fully intends his family to hold onto and run for generations to come. He may come from a wealthy family or will have worked his way from nothing to the top through hard graft. He has complete authority over whatever he does and runs a tight ship where rules must be followed. He plays by the rules himself and is honest but tough in business and romance. He sorely needs someone trustworthy to come home to, so that could be you. Don't expect him to tell you his troubles though, as he'd see that as a sign of personal weakness.

Eleventh house: His friends are what keep him grounded and give him the greatest pleasure in life. He's probably still hanging out with the friends he made at school or college and chances are they still do the same kind of things for entertainment, as he knows what he likes and likes what he knows. Acceptance will be based on his friends' opinions of you. He wants you not just to complement him but to add to his status in some way. He's not looking for arm candy, but someone who will make him proud, be his best friend and never let him down.

Twelfth house: You could be sitting next to this man at work or on the bus for years and not know that he's deeply in love with you. He's definitely the strong, silent type and you'd almost need psychic skills to know what's going on in his mind. However, it's just that it takes him a lot of time to be sure of someone. He doesn't do one-night stands or 'break up to make up' romance. Once he's decided to make his move, although it may be at a glacial speed, he'll make you his and put you on a pedestal. Trust, respect, honesty, and dignity are important to this guy. He'll rescue you, comfort you through your woes, drive you anywhere if you need a ride but never, ever show him up or ridicule him. The man is a saint but he has his pride.

Chapter 24

Who to Love if You Have Venus in Aquarius

How do you decide who you want to love forever when your mind changes every other day, if not sooner, and you thrive on surprise, variety and anything and anyone out of the ordinary? Plus you value your freedom too so do you really want to be in a relationship anyway?

No wonder love is a rolling ball of confusion for you!

Venus in Aquarius gives you a love of things, situations and people who are unconventional, but it can also make you rather stubborn so you may actually be in denial about that side of your personality. Once you give in to the fact that what you want isn't necessarily what other people want from love and life, you're halfway to finding your dream relationship.

And you have a greater chance than most to make your dreams, hopes and aspirations come true simply because of having Venus in Aquarius. It's an astrological combination which can be about making the impossible a reality, so you've really lucked out more than you know.

Bear in mind that what might work best for you is a relationship where you might not get married in the conventional sense although you and your Significant Other will definitely be recognized by society as partners. You could consider living apart together, as in each keeping your own separate homes but choosing to spend most of your quality time together. This could work brilliantly for you as there's a need for a degree of personal space and independence with Venus in Aquarius.

Or you could happily continue a long distance relationship, or potentially have a situation where you're each other's best friends forever but you're not physically intimate. Again, this may be unusual in society's eyes but not necessarily for you as friendship is the most important element of any relationship as far as you're concerned.

And whoever you hook up with must also learn to like your friends as he's going to be seeing a lot of them. This goes for you and the man you're likely to fall in love with too. He's often surrounded by pals, male and female, so if you're the jealous or possessive type (though with Venus in Aquarius it's unlikely that you are) this could be hard for you to handle.

'Going out' often means going out with a posse of people whose motto is 'the more the merrier'. Group activities are the best way to get to know the man of your dreams, plus you'll see how he interacts with others and can be sure he's not just on his best behavior to impress you.

He, like you, is likely to have an individual and eclectic style, some might even call it eccentric. You may find yourself drawn to men who shock your friends and family, and no matter how sweet and innocent you might appear on the outside your inner rebel may delight in turning up to a family gathering with a guy sporting a nose-ring and a blue Mohican haircut.

Or he could be considerably older, much younger or from a completely different culture. He may point out things that others are too polite or uncomfortable to mention, especially if he's spotted something that seems unjust or unfair. He's very community-minded and compassionate, and you may find he brings home waifs and strays, of both the human or animal kind, as he's very much on the side of the underdog.

Look at the things you love to do and that's a pretty good indication of the kind of place to be or activity to indulge in to find your ideal love match too.

You're likely to be a bit of a gadget freak so head to the nearest phone store or computer emporium and make a personal connection. You, more than most Venus sign combos, could find your true love on-line on a dating site or connect through a computer gaming site.

You may be into crowds and techno music so a festival, rave or a trip to somewhere like Ibiza could be your idea of heaven.

If it's not, think instead of joining a group where you can stand out and make a difference and an impression with your individual and often ground-breaking ideas.

The one thing you definitely won't be able to cope with in a relationship is dull routine. If you look at your dating history so far it's quite likely that you break up when the guy least expects it, though your friends will have seen it coming ages before it happens, especially if the man in your life has tried to restrict or control you.

You prefer to live on the edge of a relationship and keep things up in the air, which coincidentally is the element connected to Aquarius, so you often intellectualize love rather than give in to your deeper emotions.

You're happy to be loved and to give love, but not to own or be owned by someone even if he is Mr. Right. Find that element of freedom and you've found the man for you.

So let's keep this simple and create a list of options that you can add to your master plan at the back of the book so you can identify him when you meet him. Your love match could be:

- An IT expert
- A human rights campaigner
- A computer game designer
- A scientist
- An electrician
- An inventor
- A techno musician
- A party planner
- A magician
- A fashion designer
- Someone who has lots of different or unusual jobs

- A social worker
- An astrologer
- A radio presenter
- A modern artist

This list is by no means exhaustive and you can, and should, add some options of your own. You should be getting the picture by now. Think of the things you adore that include any form of technology, anything new and groundbreaking, computers, gadgets, whatever appeals to you as unexpected and unconventional and that's the kind of lover you should be drawing towards you, or putting yourself in a position to get closer to.

Which House is Your Venus in Aquarius Sign In?

The astrological house that your Venus sign is in tells you even more about your ideal love match. If you haven't done it already, look back at the 'Find your Venus Sign' chapter for a quick and easy way to work it out.

First house: He's a quirky dresser, nothing matches but somehow it all works. He may have a natural white streak or a bright dyed fake color in his hair, and he knows how to stand out in a crowd. Sparkling, intelligent eyes mark him out as eternally curious and interested in everything, although he may have a limited attention span.

Second house: This guy is both extremely good and extremely bad with money! By some quirk of fate he can make a small fortune but is likely to lose it all on a random investment, then recoup his losses with another spontaneous stroke of luck and inspiration. He may work for the stock market or be a maverick in a regular banking institution, or simply have extraordinary intuition about current financial trends. Life will never be dull or predictable with him, but do expect bouts of financial famine and feast.

Third house: What an incredible imagination this man has.

He probably invents words, but will more than likely love to write, read and communicate especially via the latest technology. He might be a journalist or write subtitles for TV shows. He could be an inspirational teacher, possibly of languages, or he might surprise everyone one day by writing a groundbreaking novel. He's always on the move, looking for new things to do and find out about. He may have, or had at one time, a stutter as his brain often works too fast for his mouth to keep up.

Fourth house: His home will be full of gadgets as he loves widescreen 3D TVs, amazing sound systems and every kitchen fad and gizmo there is to be had. His home may be minimalist and modern, and he's a bit of a Heston Blumenthal (quirky, inventive chef) in the kitchen, making his own variations on snail porridge and egg and bacon ice cream. He might like to move house or redecorate rather a lot.

Fifth house: He's irresistibly attractive because he's actually quite detached and aloof when it comes to love. Not a player as such, but he does like to work a room to make sure he's checked everyone out, as potential friends as well as potential love interests. He needs an inspirational conversationalist to entertain and be entertained by and new social experiences and venues make him as excited as a child with a new toy. He most likely dances to techno sounds, and romances to chill-out and trance music, but anything new will intrigue him. A bit of a risk-taker, he has a charm that can only really be appreciated once you're in his inner sanctum of friends.

Sixth house: This one loves to keep fit and healthy and will use technology to help keep him that way. Anything that gauges blood pressure, counts reps at the gym or claims to get him fit fast will be an instant purchase, and he's a sucker for TV-advertised workouts or equipment. That said, he can be quite inspired and invent his own unorthodox methods to keep in trim that actually work. He loves his work but flits between being super-organized and desperately untidy.

Seventh house: He loves you, he loves you not. That's how romance might feel with this man. One day you'll get a marriage proposal out of the blue, the next he's off on a business trip that he didn't think was worth telling you about, besides which he 'needs his space and freedom'. However, you'll be his best friend as well as his lover and partner and if you like variety in life, which chances are you do, this could be the ideal arrangement for you.

Eighth house: This man has some unusual ideas in the bedroom. Gadgets and threesomes (or more) may appeal to him as he's extremely sexually adventurous and unconventional, though he's able to separate love from lust too. He's also fascinated by life's mysteries and may be deeply into astrology. Money is hit and miss with him but he often has secret or hidden resources.

Ninth house: He may be an eccentric professor or adventurer who loves to explore new lands, or simply someone who likes to go to quirky places on vacation. He may have some unorthodox views on love and relationships, and could be a media expert whose opinion is sought on these subjects. His life philosophy may be far from mainstream and he's utterly fascinating to spend time with, discussing big ideas with friends. He'll open your mind as well as win your heart.

Tenth house: If you're looking for someone with amazing ideas and an innovative take on life then watch out for an inventor, scientist or electrician with an entrepreneurial way about him. He may happily barter rather than be paid for his skills so will fix a light fitting in return for a home-cooked meal or a massage for instance, as although he's likely to be quite successful he prefers to live by his own rules rather than follow convention. He may be from humble origins but at some stage in life could be catapulted to success. It might not last but he could reap the financial rewards of his 15 minutes of fame.

Eleventh house: Friends are the most important people in his life and he looks after them like family, and vice versa. He's an idealist and may set his heart on achieving high goals, whether it's reducing world poverty or living the kind of unorthodox lifestyle he aspires to regardless of what other people think. While he loves a crowd of friends he also values his freedom so will need time and space alone to think, create and do his own thing.

Twelfth house: He'll do anything for anyone, on a whim. Generous to a fault, he'll go without rather than see anyone else in trouble or despair as he feels a strong bond with those less fortunate than himself. He may try to hide his true self, believing that if anyone got to know him really they'd find him a bit weird and unlovable. He doesn't quite fit in anywhere but that's part of his charm. He may be an inspired poet, musician or artist, either in public (you could meet him busking on the street) or on the quiet at home, as a meditation. A little encouragement and a truly loving relationship could be the making of this romantic hero in disguise.

Chapter 25

Who to Love if You Have Venus in Pisces

Your heart rules your head when you have Venus in Pisces. The softest of the Venus sign combinations, you're also likely to be a soft touch when it comes to people in distress, lost kittens and puppies and any charitable cause that wants you to part with your cash.

In fact, that may be where love has led you a not so merry dance in the past, as you're a magnet for men who have issues, who may be needy or perhaps have addictions, which puts you in the role of both savior and martyr.

How many times have you put your own needs and wants to one side for the sake of love? A healthy relationship means being able to put yourself ahead of others at times in order to be able to look after anyone else. Think of it as being like the safety demonstration on an airplane, where parents are told to put their own life-saving equipment on first so they're in a better position to help their loved ones in the event of an emergency.

With Venus in Pisces you're a naturally caring person with a lot of love to give, but that often gets depleted as others seem to help themselves to your resources without returning the compliment, so you end up physically and emotionally drained.

The best way to deal with this is to make sure you have some quiet time to yourself to re-energize and to build up a kind of protective shield that keeps out negative energy, as you tend to pick up all too easily on other people's thoughts, feelings and vibrations.

Love and nurture yourself and your senses with massages, reflexology, soothing music, beautiful art and tranquil surroundings. Being near water is especially healing for you as Pisces is a watery sign, and better yet, all of these options provide ample opportunities to meet the man of your dreams as he's also likely to be tuned in to these things.

He could be a dream interpreter, as Pisces rules the imagination and subconscious, so you could get in touch with him by getting in touch with your own mystical side.

Or he could be a keen swimmer or a lifeguard, so head to your local pool or beach but obviously don't put yourself at risk in the water just to meet Mr. Right!

You could meet him at a retreat, or sightseeing at a monastery while you're on vacation as you're both attracted to peaceful and spiritual spaces.

Think about trying out some art sessions or an alternative dance class where you can let go of boundaries and any self-consciousness to truly express yourself, because you and he are both creative souls. He could easily be a teacher on one of these courses or simply a fellow participant.

He could be a doctor specializing in foot care, as Pisces rules the feet, or a hot salesman at your favorite shoe emporium who seems to just know exactly what style suits you.

Photography and filmmaking are glamorous areas where your paths may cross, or he might work as a guard, health worker or art therapist at a not so glamorous prison. You could get together with him at the bar (rather than behind bars) of your favorite watering hole after work, though do be cautious if he seems to drink like a fish, which is an occasional downside of Venus in Pisces.

Charity organizations where volunteering and giving selflessly are key are also places for the potential love of your life to be working or spending his spare time.

And if you love sailing, whether it's smart yachts or rowing boats, he could turn out to be the captain of your heart, not just the captain of your ship.

So let's keep this simple and create a list of options that you can add to your master plan at the back of the book so you can identify him when you meet him. Your love match could be:

- An artist
- A reflexologist
- A dancer
- A sailor
- A poet
- Someone who writes about health
- A psychotherapist
- A film maker
- An actor
- A magician
- A care worker
- A spa owner
- A hypnotist
- Someone who works on a cruise ship
- A fisherman

This list is by no means exhaustive and you can, and should, add some options of your own. You should be getting the picture by now. Think of the things you adore that include any form of art, therapy, music, dance, movies and water-related activities including fishing, swimming and spas, and that's the kind of lover you should be drawing towards you, or putting yourself in a position to get closer to.

Which House is Your Venus in Pisces Sign In?

The astrological house that your Venus sign is in tells you even more about your ideal love match. If you haven't done it already, look back at the 'Find your Venus Sign' chapter for a quick and easy way to work it out.

First house: He's got floppy hair and a faraway look in his eyes. A lopsided grin and a kind face add to the illusion of slight helplessness that makes you want to take care of him. He's a little bit hopeless but in a hopelessly romantic way. He makes your heart melt with his soft voice and lovely manners, and he reminds you of a poet from a bygone era. He's something of a lost soul but gets by with help from everyone he meets because of his natural charm.

Second house: Money is a concept that this guy hasn't quite grasped. If he has it he tends to give it away to charitable causes, but the universe is kind to him so what goes around comes around and mostly what he gives away comes back in some form or another. Call it karma if you will, but sharing good fortune seems to work for him. While he's exceedingly generous he can be taken advantage of at times, as he's a sucker for a sob story.

Third house: He's deeply romantic and loses himself in books and poems, writing them as well as reading them. Chances are he has a soft and sensual voice so would make a wonderful orator or storyteller. There's an almost hypnotic tone to the way he speaks so he can persuade anyone to do anything, including getting complete strangers to tell him details of their lives for newspaper stories if he's a journalist. He finds the point that almost breaks your heart and brings you to tears in every tale he tells or song he sings. Not averse to telling the odd fib or two to get him off the hook at times, he makes up for it with genuine and deep words of love.

Fourth house: Home is his sanctuary and safe haven. It might be quite spartan in style, as he's not big on personal comfort, but it will be a wonderful retreat. It might be near the sea or a river, or could even be on a barge or houseboat as he feels most at home on or near the water. It might even be a meditation center and will have a very special, quite serene energy. You'll feel calm and loved in this environment, but watch out for the saucy water-bed! Having a family is a very healing thing for this guy, and he'll do whatever it takes to benefit and protect his loved ones.

Fifth house: He's incredibly talented as an artist or musician, maybe a singer, perhaps all three. This makes him very alluring so expect him to be surrounded by adoring female fans. As a parent he might be a bit of a pushover and not so good with instilling discipline, but he'll help raise a family of very creative individuals. He loves the idea of love, so may be an incurable romantic. Work-wise, he may run a bar or pub.

Sixth house: This guy has natural healing ability, so he looks very good whatever his age and most likely works in an environment that promotes health in some way. Feet may be his specialty (Pisces rules the feet) so he could be a reflexologist or chiropodist. He could also be a counselor or psychotherapist as he has insight into emotional pain and making things better. Dance is another of his loves and talents. He could also work in an aquarium or be a fishmonger.

Seventh house: The ultimate romantic, this man seems to know intuitively just what you need to keep you happy, and more to the point he loves doing it. Expect wining and dining and fresh flowers, though giving you a beautiful shell from the beach you first kissed on is more his style, and foot rubs are his specialty. If you reciprocate, so much the better, but he's more of a giver than a taker. Very tactile and sensual, he loves and needs the reassurance that having you touch his face or stroke his hair gives him. He'd truly do anything for you, and the truth is you'd do the same for him.

Eighth house: There are some deep emotional bonds waiting to be formed with this man. Money, power and sensuality are like breathing to him but they're also areas of self sacrifice so never try to use any of them as weapons against him, or withhold your favors in the bedroom as a bargaining tool as this could get you both into murky psychological waters. You may find you develop an almost psychic connection where, even when apart, you each feel what the other is feeling, emotionally and sometimes physically too.

Ninth house: This man is something of a crusader who'd like to heal the world if he could. Extremely caring, he feels very deeply things such as natural disasters in underprivileged countries and may be an international care worker, wanting to be first on the scene to help out. He thinks deeply too so may also be a philosopher or college lecturer. Very spiritual, he loves to learn about alternative beliefs and may be seriously into yoga or tai chi.

Tenth house: If he's a boss, he'll be the kindest boss in the world. Generous to his staff, his only trouble may be that he ends up doing half their work to ease the load and always stays late at the office as a result. He's quite charismatic and persuasive, and may seem like a soft touch but knows when to put his foot down when he has to. He might work in the caring or health industries, on cruise ships or in the film business. If he's an artist he has the potential to be recognized for the depth and emotional quality of his work.

Eleventh house: This guy would be lost without his friends, as would they be without him. They're a little like a mutual support group so that where one goes, the others have to follow. If you hook up with him you'll need to be able to fit in with his and his friends' idiosyncrasies and be prepared to talk about your feelings, as they're quite a touchy feely bunch. He's also on a mission to achieve his most heartfelt aspirations, which could be to strive for world peace as much as it is to find the perfect pair of shoes or to be a great dancer (with a troupe rather than as a solo performer).

Twelfth house: This man gets himself into emotional tangles with love so may play things close to his chest for a while before revealing his true feelings. He wants love to be like it is in the movies so gets hurt when reality doesn't quite match his expectations. He may work in the media, as a therapist or may be very creative but a little shy about revealing his talents to others. Deeply loving, he's also highly intuitive and picks up others' moods very easily so needs some space and time to himself to recharge his batteries. He's looking for the kind of relationship where couples finish each other's sentences because they're so in tune they seem to merge.

Chapter 26

Jupiter and Your Lucky Years for Love

When you're looking for love having lucky planet Jupiter in signs that enhance your relationships can be a real bonus.

Jupiter is the planet of luck, adventure and happiness, all the good things in life, so whatever it touches gets bigger and better. If it moves through your romance and relationship signs, which it does once every 12 years, it's quite likely that a major partnership may start, or if you're in a relationship it will seem better than ever.

All you need to do is:

1. Check which are your lucky love signs below.
2. Search the list of dates to see which years are good for your relationship.

So if you're Pisces, and Jupiter is in the sign of Cancer, you're likely to be lucky in love from June 2013 to July 2014. This doesn't mean you'll fall in love with a Cancerian, but don't rule out the possibility.

Add these dates to the checklist at the back of the book to give you a better picture of when you're most likely to find love.

If Jupiter is in your own sign, you're luckier in all you do and a relationship may be a possibility, but love is more probable if Jupiter's in signs that enhance romance and partnerships.

If your sign is ARIES your love luck increases with Jupiter in LEO and LIBRA

If your sign is TAURUS your love luck increases with Jupiter in VIRGO and SCORPIO

If your sign is GEMINI your love luck increases with Jupiter in

LIBRA and SAGITTARIUS

If your sign is CANCER your love luck increases with Jupiter in SCORPIO and CAPRICORN

If your sign is LEO your love luck increases with Jupiter in SAGITTARIUS and AQUARIUS

If your sign is VIRGO your love luck increases with Jupiter in CAPRICORN and PISCES

If your sign is LIBRA your love luck increases with Jupiter in AQUARIUS and ARIES

If your sign is SCORPIO your love luck increases with Jupiter in PISCES and TAURUS

If your sign is SAGITTARIUS your love luck increases with Jupiter in ARIES and GEMINI

If your sign is CAPRICORN your love luck increases with Jupiter in TAURUS and CANCER

If your sign is AQUARIUS your love luck increases with Jupiter in GEMINI and LEO

If your sign is PISCES your love luck increases with Jupiter in CANCER and VIRGO

Jupiter Dates

2014 Jupiter is in Cancer until 15 July 2014

2014-1015 Jupiter is in Leo from 16 July 2014 to 10 August 2015

2015-2016 Jupiter is in Virgo from 11 August 2015 to 8 September 2016

2016-2017 Jupiter is in Libra from 9 September 2016 to 10 October 2017

2017-2018 Jupiter is in Scorpio from 11 October 2017 to 8 November 2018

2018-2019 Jupiter is in Sagittarius from 9 November 2018 to 19 December 2019

2019-2020 Jupiter is in Capricorn from 20 December 2019 to 16 December 2020

2020-2021 Jupiter is in Aquarius from 17 December 2020 to 28

December 2021

2021-2022 Jupiter is in Pisces from 29 December 2021 to 20 December 2022

2022-2023 Jupiter is in Aries from 21 December 2022 to 16 May 2023

2023-2024 Jupiter is in Taurus from 17 May 2023 to 25 May 2024

Chapter 27

When Venus Meets Mars: Your Hot Love Dates

When Venus and Mars meet in the same sign, or are 'conjunct' to use the technical term, love is in the air. The dates below show when your sign is most likely to find love, based on Venus and Mars encounters. These windows of opportunity tend to be quite short so use them, don't lose them.

Take another look at the 'Where to Find Love' chapter for your Sun sign and make sure you're out and about on these dates, ideally doing something connected to the options suggested for you within those pages. If you want to increase your chances of finding love, staying home alone at these times is not an option. Whatever you do, do something to put yourself out there to meet someone special.

If for some reason you really, truly can't get out of the house on these key dates you can still be proactive. Try internet dating or invite friends (and ideally friends of friends) around to your place to expand your social circle. A great relationship is waiting for you to tune in to it, so don't miss these rare and wonderful phases as they don't come along that often.

And if your sign seems to be getting a raw deal with barely a mention don't despair. The dates listed are great for every sign, but the ones getting a special mention are particularly favored on the dates shown as the dynamic duo of Venus and Mars lights up either their own sign, their romance sign or their relationship sign.

So if Venus and Mars are in Pisces, for example, Pisceans become total love magnets, Virgos may find they're irresistibly attracted to someone amazing, and Scorpios are likely to meet a soulmate who could become a lifelong partner.

One other thing to remember is that, while there's every possibility that your eyes may meet someone else's across a crowded room and it'll be love at first sight, it's more likely that someone you encounter on these special dates will click with you in a more subtle way. This relationship will develop over the coming months rather than burn out in an all-consuming passion. The exact time you meet is a 'seed' moment, starting the process for love to grow and blossom into something truly beautiful and, more importantly, long lasting.

And don't sit around feeling blue in the quiet times when Venus and Mars aren't connecting. You can also check what Jupiter is up to and whether that's affecting you, and see whether you're in a strong Venus cycle too. Remember to get on with having a meaningful and fulfilling life, whether you're in a relationship or not!

Right now, add the dates that mention your sign, your romance sign and your relationship sign to the checklist at the back of the book.

Your Romance and Relationship Signs

If your Sun sign is ARIES your romance sign is LEO and your relationship sign is LIBRA

If your Sun sign is TAURUS your romance sign is VIRGO and your relationship sign is SCORPIO

If your Sun sign is GEMINI your romance sign is LIBRA and your relationship sign is SAGITTARIUS

If your Sun sign is CANCER your romance sign is SCORPIO and your relationship sign is CAPRICORN

If your Sun sign is LEO your romance sign is SAGITTARIUS and your relationship sign is AQUARIUS

If your Sun sign is VIRGO your romance sign is CAPRICORN and your relationship sign is PISCES

If your Sun sign is LIBRA your romance sign is AQUARIUS and your relationship sign is ARIES

If your Sun sign is SCORPIO your romance sign is PISCES and

your relationship sign is TAURUS

If your Sun sign is SAGITTARIUS your romance sign is ARIES and your relationship sign is GEMINI

If your Sun sign is CAPRICORN your romance sign is TAURUS and your relationship sign is CANCER

If your Sun sign is AQUARIUS your romance sign is GEMINI and your relationship sign is LEO

If your Sun sign is PISCES your romance sign is CANCER and your relationship sign is VIRGO

Venus and Mars Dates

2015

January 4–January 11: Both planets are in the air sign Aquarius. Good for Aquarius, Leo, Libra

January 28–February 19: Both planets are in the water sign Pisces. Good for Pisces, Virgo, Scorpio

February 21–March 16: Both planets are in the fire sign Aries. Good for Aries, Libra, Sagittarius

April 1–April 11: Both planets are in the earth sign Taurus. Good for Taurus, Scorpio, Capricorn.

August 9–September 24: Both planets are in the fire sign Leo. Good for Leo, Aquarius, Aries

October 9–November 8: Both planets are in the earth sign Virgo. Good for Virgo, Pisces, Taurus.

November 13–December 4: Both planets are in the air sign Libra. Good for Libra, Aries, Gemini.

2016

December 8–December 18: Both planets in Aquarius. Good for Aquarius, Leo, Libra.

2017

January 3–January 27: Both planets in Pisces. Good for Pisces, Virgo, Scorpio.

February 4–March 9: Both planets in Aries.
Good for Aries, Libra, Sagittarius.
August 26–September 4: Both planets in Leo.
Good for Leo, Aquarius, Aries.
September 20–October 13: Both planets in Virgo.
Good for Virgo, Pisces, Taurus.
October 23–November 6: Both planets in Libra.
Good for Libra, Aries, Gemini.

2019

July 28–August 17: Both planets are in Leo.
Good for Leo, Aquarius, Aries.
August 21–September 14: Both planets are in Virgo.
Good for Virgo, Pisces, Taurus.
October 4–October 8: Both planets are in Libra.
Good for Libra, Aries, Gemini.

2021

June 3–June 11: Both planets in Cancer.
Good for Cancer, Capricorn, Pisces.
June 27–July 21: Both planets in Leo.
Good for Leo, Aquarius, Aries.
July 30–August 15: Both planets in Virgo.
Good for Virgo, Pisces, Taurus.

2022

January 25–March 5: Both planets in Capricorn.
Good for Capricorn, Cancer, Virgo.
March 6–April 5: Both planets in Aquarius.
Good for Aquarius, Leo, Libra.
April 15–May 2: Both planets in Pisces.
Good for Pisces, Virgo, Taurus.
May 25–May 28: Both planets in Aries.
Good for Aries, Libra, Sagittarius.

2023

May 8–May 20: Both planets in Cancer.

Good for Cancer, Capricorn, Pisces.

June 6–July 9: Both planets in Leo.

Good for Leo, Aquarius, Aries.

December 30–December 31: Sagittarius.

Good for Sagittarius, Gemini, Leo.

2024

January 1–January 4: Both planets in Sagittarius.

Good for Sagittarius, Gemini, Leo.

January 23–February 12: Both planets in Capricorn.

Good for Capricorn, Cancer, Virgo.

February 17–March 11: Both planets in Aquarius.

Good for Aquarius, Leo, Libra.

March 23–April 4: Both planets in Pisces.

Good for Pisces, Virgo, Scorpio.

2025

December 1–December 14: Both planets in Sagittarius.

Good for Sagittarius, Gemini, Leo.

December 25–December 31: Both signs in Capricorn.

Good for Capricorn, Cancer, Virgo.

Chapter 28

Putting it all Together: Your 'Finding Love' Checklist

Completing this checklist will give you the key dates when you're most likely to find love. If just one of these astrological ingredients is working in your favor your chances of romance are increased, and if two or more events coincide you may as well start planning the wedding!

1. Are you in a strong Venus cycle?

_____

(Are you aged 14, 21, 28, 35, 42, 49, 56, 63, 70, 77, 84, 91, 98?)

2. When is Jupiter activating your love luck?

_____

3. When are Venus and Mars together in your:

SUN SIGN _____

ROMANCE SIGN _____

RELATIONSHIP SIGN _____

4. Where do you need to be on these key dates to find love (check your Sun sign's 'Where to Find Love' chapter)?

_____

_____

_____

_____

5. What kind of guy should you look out for (check the 'Find Your Venus Sign' and 'Who to Love' chapters)?

_____

_____

_____

_____

Good luck! And don't forget to share your own romantic 'how we met' experiences at www.orlilysen.com

Dodona Books offers a broad spectrum of divination systems to suit all, including Astrology, Tarot, Runes, Ogham, Palmistry, Dream Interpretation, Scrying, Dowsing, I Ching, Numerology, Angels and Faeries, Tasseomancy and Introspection.